beading
for the Soul

INSPIRED DESIGNS FROM 23 CONTEMPORARY ARTISTS

DEBORAH CANNARELLA

INTERWEAVE PRESS
www.interweave.com

D1122896

Editor: Christine Townsend
Designer: Karen Schober
Production: Dean Howes
Photo stylist: Ann Swanson
Illustrator: Ann Swanson
Photographer: Joe Coca
Proofreader and indexer: Nancy Arndt

Text © 2005 Deborah Cannarella
Illustrations © Interweave Press LLC
Photography © 2005 Joe Coca and Interweave Press LLC, unless noted otherwise.

 Interweave Press LLC
201 East Fourth Street
Loveland, CO 80537-5655 USA
www.interweave.com

Printed in China through C & C Offset Printing Co., LTD

Library of Congress Cataloging-in-Publication Data

Cannarella, Deborah.
  Beading for the soul : inspired designs from 23 contemporary artists / Deborah Cannarella.
     p. cm.
  Includes bibliographical references and index.
  ISBN 1-931499-46-2 (pbk.)
  1. Beadwork—Patterns. I. Title.
  TT860.C365 2005
  745.58'2—dc22
                                    2005001684
10 9 8 7 6 5 4 3 2 1

For all the artists, who agreed to explore the sacred meaning of their lives and their work— and for all those inspired to do the same.

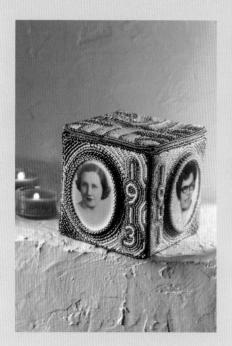

CONTENTS

chapter one
BEADING FOR PROTECTION 7

Eye Bead Necklace 10
Stephanie Sersich

Green Guardian Necklace 12
Sage Holland

Lover's Eye Pin 15
Laura McCabe

chapter two
BEADING FOR HEALING 19

Baltic Princess Necklace 22
Margi Foster

Milagros Necklace and
Shrine Pin 25
Kim Yubeta

Milagros Bracelet 30
Stephanie Sersich

Healing Journal 32
Robin Atkins

chapter three
BEADING FOR STRENGTH 37

Broadcollar Variation 40
Julia Pretl

Pinto Bear Necklace 45
Mary Hicklin

Peruvian Cat Totem Bag 50
Susan Guagliumi

Armillary and Cosmic Orbit 54
Victoria Hughes

chapter four
BEADING FOR GOOD 59

Chinese Good Fortune Pouch 62
Helen Banes

Two Fetish Bags 67
David Dean

Pearl Peace Dove Necklace 70
Isis Ray

Bead Mobile 74
Beau Anderson

chapter five
BEADING FOR PRAYER 79

Bead-Embroidered Icon 82
Mary Walker

Handheld Prayer Beads 87
Eleanor Wiley

Beaded Mandala 91
Mary Tafoya

Three Beaded Prayers 96
Sonya Clark
Stephenie Goodwin

chapter six
BEADING FOR BONDING 101

Wedding Shawl 104
Eleanor Wiley

Double-Strand Bridal Necklace 107
Laura McCabe

French Beaded Roses 112
Donna DeAngelis Dickt

Heirloom Cube 119
Julia Pretl

chapter seven
BEADING FOR REMEMBRANCE 125

Personal Symbols Neckband 128
Diane Fitzgerald

Totem Necklace 132
Chelle Mayer

Two Scarab Brooches 136
Judith Bennett

GALLERY 141

GLOSSARY OF TECHNIQUES 151

REFERENCES AND
SUGGESTED READING 157

SOURCES 158

INDEX 159

chapter one

BEADING FOR PROTECTION

We protect our bodies against the harsh elements by wearing clothing and building shelter. But how do we protect ourselves against those equally powerful, intangible threats we cannot see—whatever we might believe them to be?

From ancient times, beads have served as powerful amulets to ward off disease, unfortunate accidents, acts of sorcery, the wrath of malevolent spirits, and ill temper. Across cultures, beadworkers have relied on beads of various types, colors, and patterned designs to shield themselves from events and energies that might cause physical or psychic harm.

According to the old adage, "Beauty is in the eye of the beholder." But apparently there is more in the eye than that. The eyes, the so-called windows of the soul, are believed to have great power—for good and evil. People of many cultures believe that a person can transmit malice and envy with a hateful glance, through the power of what is known as the Evil

Eye. The glance has a destructive effect on the individual who receives it—and can rob a person of envied traits, worldly possessions, and even presence of mind. The most vulnerable, most valued members of society—pregnant women and children—are most susceptible.

One of the oldest forms of beads worn as protection against the Evil Eye is the eye bead. Eye beads typically have patterns of circles or dots that resemble or symbolize the human eye. They protect the wearer by boldly confronting and diverting the offensive glance—eye to eye—with a powerful glance cast on behalf of the wearer.

The ancient Phoenicians manufactured small sculptural head beads and mask pendants—possibly a variation on the eye bead. The Romans made face beads of colorful mosaic glass. In Africa and India, some people believe cowrie shells resemble human eyes, so children and adults wear the shells for protection.

Eye amulets were also worn to conjure the presence of a powerful, protective guardian. The people of ancient Egypt frequently wore the Eye of Horus, the god of the Heavens. According to myth, the left eye of the god was lost in a battle and magically restored. This highly stylized eye was called the *udjat*, which means "whole" or "undamaged."

In many cultures, the colors red and blue have protective power. In regions of western Asia, carnelian is effective against the Evil Eye and envy. In Ecuador, newborns wear red seed bead bracelets. In North Africa, children wear coral, which also protects dwellings from lightning and tidal waves.

In the Arab world and parts of Africa, even a single blue bead, worn or sewn onto clothing, will protect the wearer. Palestinians believe the Evil Eye is light blue in color, so women wear blue beaded embellishments. Among the Berbers of North Africa, the "good eye" is blue.

Ancient Egyptians prized blue stones, such as lapis lazuli and turquoise. Turquoise is also sacred in Iran, Tibet, and other Asian cultures, and it is

Strands of watchful eye beads peer in every direction to safeguard the wearer against any danger that approaches. In many cultures, blue is a protective color, so eye beads made of blue glass or turquoise provide even greater protection against the Evil Eye. Photo courtesy of the Bead Museum, Glendale, Arizona.

revered among southwestern Native Americans. Some early writings claim that turquoise protects people—and animals—from injury due to a fall and will change hue when danger approaches.

The golden green peridot is another stone believed to protect against the Evil Eye. Among the Chinese, jade, fashioned into the form of a padlock, is attached to an infant's neck to tether the child's spirit to life and protect against disease.

From birth, Muslims wear eye beads and other amulets to protect against the Evil Eye. The most powerful amulet is the *khamsa*, which means "five" in Arabic. It is also known as the Hand of Fatima, a reference to the daughter of the prophet Mohammed. The Israeli counterpart to this amulet is the *hamsa* or *hamesh*, which means "five" in Hebrew and is itself a protective number. Hand amulets are also found in Native American, Mediterranean, and Latin American cultures.

The Dayak of Borneo believe that beadwork protects the wearer. To keep their children safe, they attach netted beadwork to baby carriers called *ba*'. The beaded patterns may be geometric or curvilinear motifs that represent human figures, tigers, or *aso*, protective dog-dragon beings. All prevent the child's soul from being lured away by evil spirits.

Whether threats are real or imagined, lingering traces of centuries-old folk superstitions or personal demons of your own making, beaded protection can go a long way toward ensuring peace of mind. The designers in this chapter have created their own improvisations on the forms and functions of traditional protective stones and amulets. These modern-day talismans inspire each of us to consider: Just what is it we value enough to protect, how might we provide that protection—and what do we hope to protect against?

A Dayak baby carrier is decorated with a protective pattern of netted beadwork and often with bells, shells, old family beads, claws, teeth, and other charms. The jangling of the amulets repels evil spirits, and the family beads make their own specific sounds to warn the mother of danger. Photo courtesy of the Minneapolis Institute of Arts, The Fiduciary Fund (14 × 12" [35.6 × 31.8 cm]).

EYE BEAD NECKLACE

Stephanie Sersich

MATERIALS

20–30 eye bead pendants

20 sterling silver eye beads

Tube of black size 8° seed beads

2 sterling silver beads, 6.5mm, with holes large enough for 3 crimp tubes to fit inside

6 sterling silver cones or bead caps, 5×3mm

Sterling silver hook and eye clasp

6 silver crimp tubes

70" (178 cm) of .024 mm beading wire

TOOLS

Crimping pliers

Wire cutters

Alligator clip or similar

TECHNIQUES

Stringing (page 156)

Crimping (page 156)

MAKING THE NECKLACE

Cut three 23" (58.5 cm) lengths of beading wire. Attach one length of wire to the ring on the clasp.

"The first eye beads I handled came from my mother's friend Kohar, who grew up in Turkey. I was struck by the beads' irregularity and simple beauty, and was attracted to their intrinsic magic.

"I learned to make beads from Sage Holland, who explained to me the significance of eye beads in history, and I adopted the motif. I've always loved to create pieces that allow me to infuse traditional themes with my own sensibilities. I have a deep spiritual connection to all my work. Creating the beads themselves is, for me, a meditation and a ritual, and it is an honor to create objects that others deem talismanic.

"This piece is made with my own lampworked version of traditional Turkish eye beads. Figuring you can never have too much of a good thing, I loaded three strands with them. The style of this necklace subtly mimics the traditional coin necklaces found throughout the world, which symbolize a wish for fertility, abundance, and prosperity."

String 1 large silver bead and 1 silver cone from the outside in. String 1" (2.5 cm) or so of seed beads, then 1 silver or glass eye bead. The more random the placement of the eye beads, the better, but space them so you don't run out. Stop stringing when you have 18 to 20" (45.5 to 51 cm) of beads. Attach a clip to keep the beads from falling off the wire.

Repeat the process for the two remaining lengths, passing the crimped wire through the large silver bead and through a small cone. While you string the second and third strands, keep in mind that the eyes should be spread out and should not lie on top of one another when the three strands are together.

When all the strands are the same length, string a cone on each strand from the inside out. Then put all three strands through the second large silver bead. Snug the beads so that the first set of crimps are hidden. Attach each end of the wire to the clasp with a crimp tube, one wire at a time. Trim the wire and adjust the strands so the crimps are inside the large silver bead and all the strands move freely.

GREEN GUARDIAN NECKLACE

Sage Holland

"We live on a wildlife refuge in Arkansas, with more than 2,000 acres of nature's bounty to watch over in our spare time. We fill some days patrolling borders for poachers, illegal stone stealers (we live in Stone County), and loggers who often just 'mistakenly' cut across the property line. However, most days we're overloaded with other tasks and have little or no time to be the stewards that we deeply wish to be. So we need all the help we can get—mortal and divine.

"This necklace is a sacred reflection of guardian spirits, always present in the ferns, trees, creeks, rocks, mosses, flowers, and critters that live in the woods. I chose elements in various tones of green to illustrate the connections of nature to people. I've included some stones, too, such as peridot, amethyst, and jasper. I made the individual lampworked glass bead myself. I etched most of the shiny surfaces of the beads to a matte finish—to emphasize their gentle inner glow.

"The eye beads express the all-seeing, all-knowing protector. The mask bead reminds me of that wild woman in the woods, evoking her spiritual strength for backup if needed while I'm quietly sneaking up to catch the bulldozers that violate the refuge line."

MATERIALS

Mask bead, with four holes, of glass, ceramic, or polymer clay

Focal bead, slightly smaller than the mask bead

8–11mm beads and stones

Small seed beads and teardrop beads

Medium beading wire

Silk beading thread

14" (35.5 cm) of 20-gauge silver wire

Sterling silver bead cap or cone

Sterling silver hook and eye clasp

4 crimp beads

Jump ring (optional)

Small charm (optional)

Beeswax

TOOLS

Beading needle

Round-nose pliers

Crimping pliers

Flat-nose pliers

Flat metal file

Dremel tool or bead reamer (as needed)

TECHNIQUES

Stringing (page 156)

Simple fringe (page 154)

Wirework (page 153)

MAKING THE TASSEL

To make the tassel top for the center bead, you'll need a bead with four holes. This bead allows for a horizontal stringing hole and a vertical hole for the hair and chin plate. I made my mask bead out of glass, but you could make one out of polymer clay.

To start the tassle, use a beading needle to string 15 or so small seed beads on a 3' (91.5 cm) length of thread. Leave a 5" (12.5 cm) tail. Terminate each line of seed beads with a small teardrop bead and pass back through the same line of beads to make a simple fringe leg. Repeat to add twelve or more strands of beads. Finish the cluster by tying the thread ends together four times (Figure 1). Trim, leaving a 5" (12.5 cm) tail. Wax the tails so they are easier to thread through the hole in the center bead. (It helps if the bead has a slightly recessed hole so that the seed-bead cluster will fit into it for an unseen junction.)

With round-nose pliers and 8" (20.5 cm) of silver wire, make a looped hook with two parallel lengths, one 2½" (6.5 cm) longer than the other. The shorter one should be about two-thirds the length of the mask bead (Figure 2).

Catch the center of the tassle in the loop of the hook and pass the hook ends

through the hole of the mask bead, tucking in the waxed thread ends (Figure 3). Pull the long wire end gently to tighten the fit. The short length of the hook is hidden inside the bead. To finish the longer length—and form a chin cap— string the silver bead cap from inside to outside (Figure 4).

Make a wire-wrapped loop to secure the beads. File the rough edge and hammer the loop for a finished look. Or you can attach a jump ring and charm to the loop instead. Set aside.

STRINGING THE NECKLACE

Cut two lengths of beading wire, one 21" (53.5 cm) and the other 25" (63.5 cm). Pair one end of the wires together and string a crimp bead and one end of the clasp. Pass back through the crimp bead and crimp. String 4" (10 cm) of larger beads onto both wires.

Working with the shorter wire, string a 1" (2.5 cm) combination of seed beads, then 5" (12.5 cm) of larger beads. String the small focal bead and repeat the stringing sequence in reverse with the short wire only. Do not crimp yet.

On the longer wire, string 2" (5 cm) of seed beads and enough larger beads to reach the desired point under the small focal bead. String the tassel and the rest

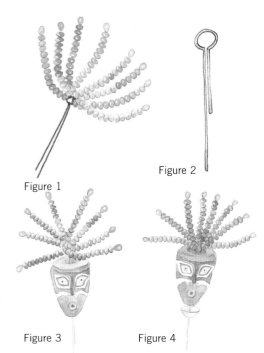

Figure 1

Figure 2

Figure 3

Figure 4

of the necklace in reverse, ending the strand by passing up through the last section of large beads added in the shorter strand. Pass both wire ends through a crimp tube and the other side of the clasp. Pass back through the crimp bead, snug the beads, and crimp.

I made a counterbalance for the back of the necklace to even out the weight of the piece. (The watchful eye bead there also helps protect the wearer.) String 1 crimp bead and 8 or so seed beads onto an 8" (20.5 cm) length of beading wire. Pass through one side of the clasp and back through the crimp bead to make a loop. Crimp. String 3" (7.5 cm) of beads, 1 crimp bead, and several seed beads to loop into the last bead. Pass back through the crimp bead and crimp.

LOVER'S EYE PIN

Laura McCabe

MATERIALS

Prosthetic or glass taxidermy animal eye (found in antique shops or online sources)

5 g each size 11° Delicas, 2 colors

10 g each size 11° Japanese seed beads, 2 colors

5 g each size 15° Japanese seed beads, 2 colors

Assorted embellishment beads (small pearls, Czech glass)

Nymo D or other beading thread in one color to match the beads and another to match the leather

2 pieces of scrap leather

Beeswax

E-6000 adhesive

Round toothpicks

Metal pin finding

TOOLS

Size 12 English beading needles

Small embroidery scissors

TECHNIQUES

Backstitch (page 155)

Tubular peyote stitch (page 153)

Looped fringe (page 155)

Whipstitch (page 155)

"The tradition of wearing eye jewelry to ward off evil spirits and the ill will of others is ancient in its origins, dating back at least 4,000 years to the people of Mesopotamia. A more recent, and intriguing, take on this ancient tradition is the 'lover's eye,' popular during England's Georgian period. In the early nineteenth century, it was fashionable to have a portrait of your lover's eye painted on ivory and set in jewelry. The most common form was a pin, worn by men at the collar or on a waistcoat or by women as a brooch, although lover's eyes are also found in rings and pendants of the period. Because each person's eye is unique, the wearer could carry an accurate portrait close to the heart, without revealing the lover's identity to others. In this way, too, the lover would always be watching over the wearer.

"This piece is a modern-day take on the intriguing Georgian tradition. Although the pin is made with an antique human prosthetic (matching the eye color of your lover), it can also be made with glass taxidermy animal eyes."

MAKING THE PIN

Trace the perimeter of the eye onto a piece of leather. Trim the leather ⅜" (1 cm) from the line. Trace the leather circle onto a second piece of leather and trim. Cut two openings in one of the leather circles to accommodate the pin finding.

With a toothpick, apply an even coat of adhesive to the edges of the eye. Glue the eye to the center of the leather circle (the one without the openings) and let dry. Knot the end of a 5 to 6' (152.5 to 183 cm) length of waxed thread and pass the needle through the leather from the wrong side so it exits right next to the eye. Work a foundation round at the base of the eye with backstitch and Delicas. Make sure that you finish with an even number of beads. Weave through the entire perimeter of the beads one more time to ensure good tension.

Work two rounds of tubular peyote stitch upward from the base round with Delicas until you reach the curve in the eye. Switch to size 15° beads.

The decrease in bead size will cause the bezel to curve inward and create a tight fit to the eye.

When you have made the bezel as high as you would like, weave the thread back through the beads to the base row, pass through the leather, and make a knot close to the surface.

Pass up through the leather and backstitch a second base row of Delicas around the edge of the bezel. As before, end with an even number of beads. Pass through the entire row one more time, stitch back through the leather, and knot to secure.

Start a new thread that is the same color as the leather. Pass up through the leather between the bezel and the outer base row and set aside.

The second piece of leather will cover the back of the pin. Work the pin finding up through the two holes so just the clasp and pin end poke up through to the right side of the leather. With a toothpick, apply adhesive to the underside of the bezeled cabochon, taking care not to glue the thread hanging from the top of the work. Place the wrong sides of the two leather circles together and press to ensure even contact. Allow to dry for at least ten minutes.

Cut away any excess leather, leaving a small edge about the width of a row of Delicas. To ensure that the backing does not pull away and to finish the edge, whipstitch the entire perimeter with the thread that is still attached to the piece.

Pass the needle back up through both pieces of leather and through a couple of beads in the outer base row. Now work tubular peyote stitch to cover the leather edge. Stitch one round of Delicas followed by two rounds of size 11° beads. On the final round, instead of picking up only one size 11° before passing through the next bead, pick up several, along with other embellishment beads if you wish. This technique will create a looped fringe. I usually create smaller loops of beads along the top side of the pin, gradually increasing the number as I approach the center bottom, and decreasing as I come up again to the top.

Finish off the thread by half-hitching several times within the work before trimming the tail.

chapter two

BEADING FOR HEALING

The soothing, rhythmic, repetitive process of beading can itself be therapeutic—a way to calm the body, channel energy, focus the mind. But the beads we select and the objects we make can be just as significant for our sense of well-being.

Myths, folklore, and modern superstitions all allude to the medicinal or beneficial properties of various beads and charms. In the past, those who sought healing—or who aspired to heal others—have worn, carried, or relied on these talismans to assist and empower them.

Following precise recipes, the ancients ground stones and gems—jade, pearl, and others—into powders to make healthful potions. Other stones reputedly drew healing powers from their colors or physical characteristics.

The ancient Egyptians, who greatly valued blue stones, believed lapis lazuli cured eye ailments. During the Middle Ages, people believed lapis ensured healthy limbs. Rubies, carnelians, and other red stones were cures for blood disorders and inflammation. Yellow stones, such as topaz, remedied jaundice and liver disease. Emeralds were aids to eyesight and antidotes to snakebites.

The people of ancient Egypt also believed that hematite, a red oxide of iron, could cure headaches, inflammation, and blood and heart diseases. Others claimed the mineral drew illness out of the body. Modern mystics consider hematite "grounding" and a salve for confusion, stress, and anxiety.

Shamanic rituals in the Americas, Asia, and Australia often feature quartz crystals. Some people believe that the crystal form both draws in and sends out energy, and so can balance energies within the body. Leonardo da Vinci claimed that amethyst, a form of quartz, increases intelligence, and the Greeks believed the wine-colored stone ensured sobriety. Some people wear amethyst to detoxify the body or heighten intuitive powers.

The ways of healing are mysterious, wrapped in ritual and secret practices. Often, they are wrapped in beads, too. Beaded bags and bottles hint at—and increase the potency of—the powerful and magical healing objects and potions within. The Midewiwin, a secret society of Native American healers established in the Great Lakes region during the seventeenth century, rely on beaded sashes, shoulder bags, and charm bags in their rituals. They consider the *megis*, a type of cowrie shell, especially sacred and powerful and incorporate the shells into their designs.

Osanyin is the Yoruba god of healing and also the god of beads. Diviners known as *akapo*, or "carriers of bags," keep their magical implements in heavily beaded pouches. The colors and patterns convey the extent of the diviner's knowledge and ability. Yoruba kings carry beaded bottles that contain healing liquids mixed with roots, leaves, and other sacred substances. The magical contents are known only to the ruler and to the healer or diviner who prepared them.

Birds, symbols of spiritually powerful women, often surround the healing and protective medicines in the beaded crowns and bottles of the Yoruba rulers of Nigeria. Birds are also a common motif on herbalists' staffs and diviners' beaded bags. Photo courtesy of the UCLA Fowler Museum of Cultural History. Photo by Don Cole (13" [33 cm]).

Traditionally, the power to heal has been reserved for shamans, medicine men, alchemists, priests, doctors, and other privileged members of society. In many cultures, however, individuals have found simple ways to directly access that invaluable power.

A *milagro*, the Spanish word for "miracle," is a small charm that serves as a votive object, a request for healing made to a particular saint or deity. It also serves as a grateful acknowledgment of healing received. Votive charms are a traditional feature of the folk art of Mexico, Ireland, and many Central, South American, and European countries.

Early milagros were made of clay, wood, and bone; later, they were cut from gold, copper, silver, and tin. The small amulets frequently represent body parts and may be simple or ornate in design—and sometimes are anatomically correct. A petitioner may pin a milagro to a statue of a saint, hang it on a painted icon, or wear the amulet until the healing occurs.

Statues covered with milagros are a frequent sight in churches, hospitals, and roadside shrines in Mexico and the American Southwest. Often pinned to the charms are photographs of loved ones or notes with special requests or expressions of thanks. Some churches sell or keep a supply of milagros as they might votive candles. When the statues are completely covered, the milagros are removed and recycled for the next group of hopeful pilgrims.

A milagro may represent a physical ailment or a spiritual one. A person who has lost a loved one or who has had heart surgery may wear a heart milagro to request an easing of his grief or a quick recovery. A person who values working with her hands and wishes to improve her skills may wear a hand milagro—as might a person who hopes to find a way to help a friend.

In many folk cultures, people who seek healing, of body or soul, wear small votive charms. Depending on the need, the charms may resemble eyes, lungs, hands, and legs—or trucks, taxis, and burros. Votive charms are also known as milagros. *The* milagros *shown here are from Peru, Mexico, Italy, and Greece. From the collection of Kim Yubeta.*

Healing rituals, implements, and potions notwithstanding, the power to heal may just as likely come from within—and the very process of beading may play a significant part. As the work of the designers featured in this chapter suggest, beads and stones and charms hold just as much power as you yourself give them, and that is often more than enough.

BALTIC PRINCESS NECKLACE

Margi Foster

"Amber is believed to greatly enhance—and even engender—good health and a sense of well-being in the wearer. North African tribes have long treasured amber in the belief that it has the power to cure illness. I experienced this power myself some years ago while fighting a particularly tenacious bout of flu.

"I was bedridden and ached all over. Having exhausted every other remedy I knew of, I remembered what I had heard about the healing effects of amber. I always loved collecting and working with amber and, during my many travels around the world, had accumulated a very large treasure trove. I pulled out strands of amber of all different sizes and hues and surrounded my bed with them, even placing some under my pillow. I felt good just handling it! I have never questioned whether the subsequent healing a couple of days later was a direct result of my immersion in amber, but it worked for me.

"The Greek name for amber is *elektron*. When rubbed vigorously, amber gives off an electrical charge strong enough to pick up a piece of paper. Unlike other gems, amber is warm to the touch and feels quite comfortable and comforting when worn next to the skin.

"There are many different colors of amber, ranging from milky white and honey gold to deep brown, cherry red, olive green, and black. Rare blue amber is found in the Dominican Republic, notably in Porta Plata, once a volcanic region. For this necklace, I chose a fiery red amber, which I've accented with hematite, a mineral that is also said to have healing properties—one of which is stopping hemorrhaging. Hematite is an oxide of iron and has red streaks when abraded or shattered. Its name comes from the Greek word *haima*, which means "blood." Iron is associated with Mars, the Roman god of war, and soldiers rubbed their bodies with hematite before going into battle. Upon their return, if they were wounded, hematite was used to stop the bleeding.

"Amber is actually a fossil, the solidified resin of tree sap. For me its essence gives it a great kinship with shells, which are as old as the ocean itself. This shell, which I brought back from Poland, is indigenous to the waters of the Balkans. Because much of the world's best amber comes from the Baltic Sea area around Poland, the combination of the amber and shell in this necklace has special significance for me."

MAKING THE NECKLACE

Drill a hole on each side of the shell. Make the holes large enough to accommodate the jump rings and allow a little play so the rings can move freely. Drill gently and slowly, frequently dipping the tip of the drill in water or lubricating oil to avoid shattering the shell. Attach a jump ring to each hole and set aside.

Cut three 24" (61 cm) lengths of beading wire. Knot the end of one wire and glue the knot to secure. Let dry. Pass the wire through a knot cup (from the inside out) and close the cup around the knot. String beads on the wire, randomly alternating the amber and hematite. When you have at least 1" (2.5 cm) or more of beading wire left, string a knot cup from the outside in. Tie a knot at the end of the wire and glue the knot to secure. Let dry and close the cup around the knot. Repeat this step for the remaining two strands.

Cut two 4" (10 cm) lengths of sterling silver wire. Make a wrapped loop on

one end. Use the knot cups to connect one end of each beaded strand to the loop. Pass the wire through 1 cone (from the inside out) and make a simple loop to secure the beads inside the cone. Twist the three beaded strands together in rope fashion. The twist will shorten the necklace to about 19" (48.5 cm). Connect the remaining end in the same way you did the first end.

Attach the hook side of the clasp to one end of the necklace. Attach the other end of the necklace to one of the jump rings on the shell. Use the shell's other jump ring and the hook as the closure.

MILAGROS NECKLACE AND SHRINE PIN

Kim Yubeta

"For the past fifteen years, my husband, David, my son Jake, and I have been volunteer workers for the Southwest Mission Research Center's three-day tours to the Kino missions in northern Sonora, Mexico. On one of our first trips to the church in San Ignacio Sonora, we saw a statue covered with small metal, silver, and gold eye charms tied on with strings and ribbons. When I asked about the charms, the sacristan who tends the church explained that the statue was of Saint Lucia, the patron saint of eyes and eyesight. The faithful had brought these small charms, called milagros, as offerings to petition the saint for a favor or thank her for a favor granted. There were eye milagros petitioning the saint to heal eye ailments, leg milagros for leg ailments, and heart milagros for heart ailments.

"I was hooked! As I continued my travels in Mexico, I checked the vendor's tables outside of churches and religious stores and purchased all the milagros available. I found them for sale at church gift shops like the one at San Xavier Mission in Tucson (where they are removed from the statues and recycled when supplies get low) and at yard sales in San Diego, California. Through the years, I've collected milagros that represent all the body parts—heads, torso, lungs, hands, arms, legs—including realistic and romantic versions of the human heart. I've also found milagros of cars, trucks, planes, livestock, horses, dogs, even a martini glass (which I suppose would be used to ask for help with abstinence). Eventually I began incorporating milagros into my jewelry.

"I found the sterling silver milagros for this necklace during a long-awaited trip to Oaxaca, Mexico. They are modern interpretations of the older styles found there. The hand milagros symbolize creativity and the lending or receiving of a hand when needed. The heart is a symbol of love and faith. I added small beaded bracelets to some of the hands just for fun. The Oaxacan sterling cross pendant with attached milagros is a contemporary piece made from old Oaxacan molds. The nineteenth-century Italian white-heart trade beads represent red coral. To increase healing power, they are combined with Chinese turquoise, citrine, carnelian, amber, jade, lapis,

amethyst, and old silver and copal amber from Tibet. The pure silver cross and melon beads are from the hill tribes of Thailand.

"People in Latin America, Spain, and many other regions also display milagros in their homes. They set aside a special place as a home altar or shrine, where they display photos of loved ones, candles, and other meaningful objects. These altars provide a sense of peace and comfort and a way to feel connected with a significant deity.

"From these home altars I got the idea to create what I call shrine cupboards—painted boxes covered with prayer cards, crosses, Mexican paper flowers, rhinestones, and milagros. My shrine pins were the natural progression from the cupboards—the same idea on a much smaller scale and wearable, too. The large tin Peruvian cow milagro and the small Mexican silver milagros in the shrine pin are old pieces."

MATERIALS

4–10mm glass and semiprecious stone beads in various colors, types, and shapes

Size $8°$ seed beads in several colors

2 rondelle 8mm stone beads

Various sizes and types of cross beads

Sterling silver milagros

Sterling silver cross or other focal piece

Sterling silver S-hook clasp

Nylon upholstery thread in color of choice

Clear-drying adhesive (I used Bond Adhesive 527)

TOOLS

Rouge cloth

Beading needle

Scissors

TECHNIQUES

Stringing (page 156)

Knots (page 151)

MAKING THE NECKLACE

Before assembling the necklace, polish the silver milagros and beads with the rouge cloth.

Make several small loops with 8 to 10 seed beads and attach a milagro to each one. Knot the ends of each loop and glue the knot with adhesive. Create a loop for each milagro you wish to include.

This necklace is made with four strands of graduated lengths: 24", 26", 28", and 30" (61 cm, 66 cm, 71 cm, and 76 cm).

To allow for knots every couple of inches, cut each length of thread twice as long as you wish the finished strand to be. Frequent knotting is important: If the necklace should break, the knots will prevent you from losing every bead. The knots also help ensure that the beads stay tight during years of wear. Cut enough thread to work on the shortest strand first, leaving a 6" (15 cm) tail. String 4" (10 cm) of seed beads and a few assorted beads, interspersing the milagro loops among the beads. String the second strand, building on the first strand's components to guide you. Working this way helps you determine the best placement of the larger beads and milagros. Repeat this process to string the two remaining strands. On the longest strand, add the focal piece in the center.

With an overhand knot, tie together the four loose thread ends on one end of the necklace. Pull the knot tight and add a drop of adhesive. When the glue is dry, cut off all but one thread as close to the knot as possible.

Working at the other end of the necklace, pull the beads on each strand so that they are snug. Knot the four strands together as before. Glue the knot and trim three of the strands. There will be one long thread left on each end of the necklace.

On one of the long thread ends, string 1 stone rondelle, 1 round 6mm, and 1 round 5mm bead. Snug the beads to hide the knot. Pass the thread end through one half of the clasp and back through the 5mm bead. Pull the thread tight and knot twice. Glue the knot, let it dry, and cut the thread close to the knot. Repeat for the other side of the necklace, adding the other half of the clasp.

MATERIALS

3 x 4" (7.5 x 10 cm) milagro or charm

Small milagros or charms

Assorted accent beads

6 x 6" (15 x 15 cm) balsa wood (for a finished size of 3 x 4" [7.5 x 10 cm])

Pin back

Heavy thread or nylon upholstery thread in color of choice

Clear-drying adhesive (I used Bond Adhesive 527)

Acrylic paint in color of choice

TOOLS

Craft knife

Small paintbrush

Pushpin or nail

TECHNIQUES

Knots (page 151)

Fringes (page 154)

Stringing (page 156)

MAKING THE PIN

Draw the desired shape of the pin on balsa wood and cut out the shape with the craft knife. Paint the surface of the pin. When the paint has dried thoroughly, center a large milagro or charm on the front of the wood and glue it in place. Let the glue dry.

With the pushpin, make evenly spaced holes along the bottom edge of the wood. Fold a 10" (25.5 cm) length of thread in half, pass the fold through one of the holes on the wood, and tie a lark's head knot. Repeat for each hole.

String small beads onto each loose thread end to make simple fringe. Then add a small milagro or charm to each thread. Tie a strong knot to hold the beads and milagro in place, then glue the knot.

Secure the pin back to the back of the wood with adhesive.

MILAGROS BRACELET

Stephanie Sersich

MATERIALS

25–30 silver or pewter charms

60 assorted beads (I used a combination of lampworked, silver, and gemstone beads)

6 sterling silver 6mm 14-gauge unsoldered jump rings

Sterling silver toggle clasp

8–10" (20.5–25.5 cm) of beading wire

2 silver crimp tubes

TOOLS

Crimping pliers

Round-nose pliers

Wire cutters

TECHNIQUES

Stringing (page 156)

Crimping (page 156)

"Milagros have been used for special blessings for thousands of years in different cultures throughout the world. Each charm has a special meaning, and several can be combined to make a truly unique and significant talisman for the wearer. Because milagros are thought to imbue the wearer with special healing powers, this bracelet makes a good gift for an ailing friend.

"Not all the charms in this bracelet are traditional milagros. My contemporary vision includes other types of charms. I inherited a passion for plants and flowers from my mom, and the flower charms keep me connected to her and to the earth. The hand and arm milagros are representative of the work I do with my hands, which I feel a strong need to care for and protect.

"I love the sound of the charms clinking together. The arrangement of multiple elements on a single piece really allows for individuality and personalization. What I also love about this piece is that it could just as easily grace a door or a window as a person's wrist."

MAKING THE BRACELET

Separate the charms into six groups, balancing the sizes and shapes in each group. Sort the charms, working with one group at a time. Notice the orientation of the loop on each charm. The charms that have a loop that can be strung side-to-side will lie flat on the beading wire. String the charms with perpendicular loops on an open jump ring so they all face the same direction. Make sure the charms are layered so they are all visible and close the ring.

Attach the wire to the ring side of the clasp with a crimp tube. String a heavier charm as a weight to ensure that the back (clasp side) of the bracelet doesn't move around to the front. String 5 or 6 assorted small beads. String the first group of charms (including the charms on the jump ring) and several more beads. Continue stringing groups until the bracelet is the proper length. Finish with a crimp tube and the other side of the clasp. Pass back through the tube. Before you crimp the wire, make sure the last bead is small enough to allow you to fasten the toggle. Snug the beads, crimp the tube, and trim the wire.

HEALING JOURNAL

Robin Atkins

"One day, journaling in a 'stream of consciousness' style, I surprised myself with a long list of 'commandments' about money: Thou shall never borrow money; Thou shall never have enough money; Thou shall never trust people about money. The list went on for several pages. I already knew I had money issues. I'd even gone to a counseling seminar about money fears. But, here they were, big time, in my face.

"So the next day, as I was teaching a bead embroidery class, I chose a piece of striped silk and took a $5 bill out of my purse. Without trying to figure it out, I just let the list I wrote the day before rest in the back of my mind as I began sewing beads on the silk fabric backed by the $5 bill. (I've often wished I had used a $100 bill!) When I look at the work now, I see all sorts of interesting things—the button with an anchor on it (money fears weighing me down), lines that look like a chart of stock market values, a glass cabochon that looks like a web (a trap) and reminds me of the portraits on American paper currency. But at the time, I just sewed improvisationally, allowing the process to uncover the truths within me.

"Eventually, I decided to place my bead embroidery in the cover of a handmade journal. To make the flyleaf pages, I joined $2 bills together with running stitches. It was therapeutic to use these bills because I had hoarded them for years thinking they would someday have collector value. I cut up $5, $10, and $20 bills and incorporated them with beads and other ephemera in collage pages inside the book, rubber-stamping the commandments I had written. Cutting and pasting with money really helped to heal the notion that money is precious and important. I also wrote down some of the pointers I had learned in the counseling seminar. With every stitch, every bead, and every written word, my anxiety and worries about money grew less bothersome.

"I still work on this project from time to time when my issues about money resurface. But the beading and book, even with blank pages still to be filled, have already changed my life significantly. I am more generous and trusting, less fearful, and more able to make decisions that involve financial risk.

MATERIALS

Small piece of new or used fabric

Small piece of lightweight acid-free paper, such as interleaving paper

Assorted seed and bugle beads

Assorted ephemera, charms, buttons, accent beads

Glass or stone cabochon (optional)

Size 11° and 14° seed beads

Blank book or sketchbook

Decorative medium- to heavyweight paper the same size as the book cover (optional)

Nymo D or other beading thread

PVA glue or other acid-free craft glue

Double-sided tape

TOOLS

Beading needle

Scissors

Awl or pushpin

Metal ruler

Cutting mat

Matte knife or box cutter

Small piece of fine- or medium-grade sandpaper

Small towel, folded

TECHNIQUES

Bead embroidery (page 155)

"Many people have used diaries and journals to record their most private thoughts, their secret desires, their harsh self-criticisms, and their hopes for the future. Through the process of recording these things, decisions and changes for the better frequently happen.

"If you are making this project for yourself for the purpose of healing, keep in mind that it does not have to be perfect. It does not have to be art or artistic. It does not have to be correct in any way. The more that you allow yourself freedom to make 'mistakes' and the more you can let go of controlling and planning the finished look, the more likely it is that the process of making the journal will be a healing experience."

BEADING THE COVER

Begin by journaling about a specific issue. Tell the story about when you first became aware of the issue and perhaps the unspoken rules that govern your behavior around it. When you run out of things to write, it's time to begin beading. Select a piece of fabric and an assortment of beads that "feel" right, that are somehow related to your issue.

To stabilize the work as you sew, back the fabric with lightweight acid-free paper, such as the interleaving paper that museums use for archival storage of textiles. (U.S. paper currency is also acid-free.)

Draw a rectangle or square on the paper. Following the shape, baste the paper to the wrong side of the fabric with a thread of a contrasting color. The basting lines on the right side of the fabric are your beading guide. Allow a 1" (2.5 cm) fabric margin around the shape and trim the excess (Figure 1).

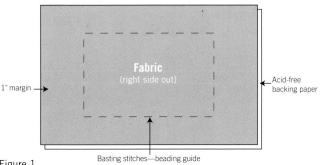

Figure 1

Figure 2

Bead the shape with various embroidery stitches. Work without a planned design. Begin sewing on beads, perhaps starting in one corner or outlining the shape in backstitch. Add buttons, charms, coins, or bits of torn paper currency.

If you'd like to add a glass or stone cabochon, place a piece of doubled-sided tape on the back of the cabochon and adhere it to the fabric, making sure there is a minimum $\frac{1}{8}$" (3 mm) margin around it.

Pass up through the fabric next to the cabochon. String 1 or 2 size 11's and 1 size 14° (the bead stack shouldn't be higher than the cabochon). Pass back through the size 11's, down through the fabric, and back up next to the beads just placed. Continue making stacks all the way around the cabochon. Sew through the beads of the first stack, exiting at the top bead. Remove the tape from the cabochon and place the cabochon back in the center of the bead stacks.

Pass through all the size 14's (including the one you exited from) to secure the cabochon. Sew down through the adja-

cent stack and tighten the thread. Knot the thread on the underside of the fabric (Figure 2).

FINISHING THE BOOK

Be sure your book has a stiff cover and a binding that allows the cover to open flat. If you plan to add collage to the pages, make sure the book has spacer strips to allow for extra thickness.

Remove any excess backing paper from around the basting stitches. The paper under the beading remains in place. Fold under the fabric borders and position the beadwork on the outside front cover of the book. With the awl or pushpin, make a small mark in the book cover at each corner of the beadwork. Remove the beadwork and connect the marks with a pencil and ruler to form a box.

Working with the cutting mat, matte knife, and ruler, carefully cut out the box. Do not cut all the way through with one stroke. Sand and smooth the edges of the opening and the cutout piece. Fit the beadwork into the opening from the inside cover, adjusting

the size as needed either by sanding or adding rows of beads.

Brush a light coat of glue on the cutout piece. Let the glue set until it is slightly tacky, then adhere it to the back of your beadwork.

Place the folded towel on your work surface. Open the book cover so it rests on the towel. Insert the beadwork through the opening from the inside of the cover. Make sure the back of the embroidery is flush with the surface. Apply glue under the fabric borders and, when the glue is tacky, smooth the fabric in place (Figure 3).

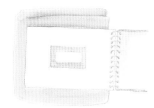

Figure 3

Trim the sheet of decorative paper so it is $\frac{1}{4}$" (6 mm) smaller than the inside cover. Center the paper and draw around it. Remove the paper and lightly brush glue within the marked area, including the cutout piece and the fabric. Allow the glue to dry until it's tacky and press the paper in place.

chapter three

BEADING FOR STRENGTH

Surely, strength comes both from within and without. Who has not had the sensation of somehow feeling better—more confident, more like one's self—when wearing a favorite color, a dazzling garment, or a meaningful memento? The ability to affect your state of mind, and that of others, through your outer appearance is a powerful psychological tool—and one that people have long integrated into their belief systems and ritualistic practices.

In many traditional African cultures, rulers and members of the royal family and court wear beads to display their high rank and importance. Their heavily beaded garments and accessories clearly identify them within their societies—and make them appear even more grand, remote, and impressive to the other members.

The Kuba people of the Democratic Republic of the Congo (Zaire) consider the king a divine being with supernatural powers. One of the king's most significant costumes is the heavily beaded *bwaantshy*, which can weigh as

The yet *belt is part of the ceremonial costume worn by a Kuba king and the royal family. The number of pendants conveys the individual's rank. This belt carries twenty-three objects: amulets decorated with glass beads and cowrie shells, miniature versions of royal hats, a ram's head, shells, and a double gong. White and blue beads signify leadership. Cowrie shells are a symbol of status.* Photo courtesy of the Minneapolis Institute of the Arts, the Ethel Morrison Van Derlip Fund (25 × 24" [63.5 × 60.96 cm]).

much as 150 pounds. Hat, tunic, belt, jewelry—even gloves and shoes—are covered with beads and cowrie shells worked in geometric motifs. The outfit provides the king with a canvas on which to display his enormous bead collection, itself a privilege reserved for royalty.

The patterns, the beads, and the colors of the beads each have symbolic meaning for the Kuba. Cowrie shells are a sign of authority and wealth. White and blue beads signify spiritual purity, high social status, and leadership. The ceremonial costume, of the king's design, is so closely tied to his identity that he is buried in it when he dies.

The beaded, multicolored crown of the Yoruba ruler signifies his stature. The crown actually empowers the king, as it both asserts his divine power and contains it. Each bead color is associated with a particular god. The faces in the designs represent royal ancestors who are spiritually linked to the ruler. Potent, secret substances are concealed in the top. A veil of beads conceals the ruler's face, which is too sacred to be exposed to view and too powerful to be looked upon by others.

In the culture of ancient Egypt, men and women of wealth and social status wore a decorative collar called a *wesekh*, meaning "broad one." The broadcollar was made of multiple rows of gold, lapis lazuli, and turquoise beads and other valued stones. Some collars also had the protective Eye of Horus amulet.

Broadcollars played an important role in Egyptian culture. The Egyptians believed that the collars, like other types of jewelry, conferred superhuman powers on the members of royalty who wore them. Archaeologists have found broadcollars in the excavated tombs of Tutankhamen and other rulers. Deities depicted on ancient sculpture, painting, and other artifacts often wear broadcollars.

In some cultures, strength came not from an elaborate costume or piece of jewelry, but rather from a simple amulet believed to have special powers that it would bestow upon the wearer. Native Americans greatly revered animals, which were essential to native life and culture. In many tribes, animal teeth, bone, and claws served as status symbols and as trophies, proof of physical strength and hunting prowess. Hunters often carried carved or natural amulets to empower and protect them. The amulet would grant the hunter the same attributes—courage, cunning, endurance—possessed by the animal to which the body part once belonged.

The Zuni, a Pueblo tribe of the American Southwest, are known for small amulets called fetishes. A fetish is a piece of stone that is either naturally formed or hand-carved to resemble a particular animal. According to Zuni myth, naturally formed fetishes are animals that twin gods struck with lightning and turned to stone so that the creatures could help mankind. The Zuni believe that the spirits of these animals are held within the naturally formed stones. A medicine man must bless fetishes that have been carved by hand, however, before they have any power.

The animal spirit residing in the fetish will share its supernatural powers with the owner only if the owner feeds it (corn meal and ground turquoise) and treats it with respect. Often, the fetish maker attaches a medicine bundle—an offering of shells, stones, or arrowheads—to increase the fetish's power. Traditionally, the owner carries the fetish in a pouch or strings it on a necklace with heishi, round shell beads. Since prehistoric times, the Zuni have carved fetishes from many types of materials, including alabaster, serpentine, jet, and turquoise.

Often, beaded objects and amulets draw their power from others' perceptions. Strength is equated with power, status, and wealth. Or an amulet's potent magic is granted by divine or supernatural intervention. The contemporary bead artists in this chapter have created empowering and empowered pieces that reveal the great strength that can come directly from the deep reserves within.

Broadcollars were popular jewelry items among ancient Egyptians of social standing—both in life and in death. The funerary pieces were often made of faience, an ancient, man-made material associated with immortality and rebirth. This wesekh *was found in the tomb of Ptahshepses Impy, an official of the Sixth Dynasty.* Photo © 2005 Museum of Fine Arts, Boston. Harvard University-Boston Museum of Fine Arts Expedition, 13.3086. 6⅞ × 6⅞ × 1" (17.4 × 17.4 × 2.5 cm).

BROADCOLLAR VARIATION

Julia Pretl

"Springtime is special to me. The hot, oppressive days of summer and the sterile cold of winter stale quickly, but spring is short and ever changing. The landscape transforms rapidly. Brown becomes green. Naked twigs are adorned with buds, which, in turn, blossom into lush abundance. Spring is both delicate and powerful. I feel new in the spring and, in an attempt to move my beadwork into a more expressive direction, I wanted my collar to convey the same sensation.

"Although it was late fall when I beaded *April*, I tried to imagine springtime—to create something airy and light yet powerful that could transform me whenever I wear it. Initially I was not happy with my choices. Pale pink and lime green are a deviation from my usual color scheme, and the netting made the necklace seem too sparse, but I pushed on.

"As I added beads, my attraction to this collar grew. It just felt right. Encircling my neck, the beads remind me of springtime. The tiny buds brush against my back and shoulders as the pale green leaves sweep across my chest, just within view. In creating this piece, I underwent the transformation that I hoped for, but the process surprised me. Not only did I achieve my goal—to create a piece that conveyed the feelings of the rebirth of spring—I also learned to let my mind abandon what it knows and allow my intuition to take over and lead."

MATERIALS

2 g per inch size 2 (6mm) matte medium pink/brown bugle beads

1¾ g per inch size 11° metallic purple seed beads (A)

2 g per inch size 11° chartreuse seed beads (B)

2½ g per inch size 11° pale pink seed beads

¾ g per inch size 8° matte metallic purple seed beads

18" (45.5 cm) strand 4mm freshwater pearls

15 pressed-glass leaves, 15 × 10mm

1" (2.5 cm) sterling silver S-hook or other clasp

2 sterling silver 8mm soldered jump rings

2 sterling silver 6mm unsoldered jump rings

Size D Nymo beading thread or 6–8 lb fishing line

12 × 12" (30.5 × 30.5 cm) flat, sturdy, cardboard box

8½ × 11" (21.5 × 28 cm) sheet of paper

TOOLS

Compass

Size 12 beading needles

Straight pins with balls on one end

Measuring tape

TECHNIQUES

Ladder stitch (page 152)

Fringes (page 154)

PREPARING THE WORK SURFACE

Measure the circumference of the base of your neck, adding about ½" (1.3 cm) for comfort. Fold the sheet of paper lengthwise and crease at the fold. Unfold and then fold and crease widthwise. Place the point of the compass at the intersection of the folds and draw a circle with the same circumference as your neck. Tape the paper to the broad side of the box. For the clasp allowance, choose a point as the top of the circle and make marks on the line ½" (1.3 cm) to each side of the center fold.

MAKING THE LADDER

Tie a tension bead 18" (45.5 cm) from the end of a 6 to 8' (182 to 244 cm) length of thread. Pick up 1A, 1 bugle, and 1B. Repeat until half the thread is strung with beads.

Separate the last segment (seed, bugle, seed) and pass through the previous segment (Figure 1).

Continue this ladder stitch until you reach the end of the strung beads (Figure 2). Slide the tension bead as necessary to allow room for the ladder to grow. If at some point you have only 6" (15 cm) of thread on either end of the last segment of the ladder, but have not yet added all the segments to the ladder, simply remove the remaining beads and end the ladder. When you're finished, secure the thread and trim close to the work.

PINNING THE FIRST LADDER

Align the top edge of one ladder end with one of the marks you made at the top of the paper circle. Carefully place a pin through the thread running between the first two bead segments (every inch or two) just below the outer thread and into the circle line. Allow the ladder to curve along the outside of the circle (don't stretch it—let the ladder lie naturally) and pin both edges every inch or so. The ladder will not yet be long enough to reach the second mark at the top of the circle but, by pinning it into position, you will see how many more sections are needed. Unpin the ladder and continue extending it until it is the correct length, keeping in mind the proper order of seed beads. When you're finished, secure the threads and trim close to the work. Repin the ladder to the circle.

NETTING AND PICOTS

Using the center fold in the paper as a reference, find the bead segment closest

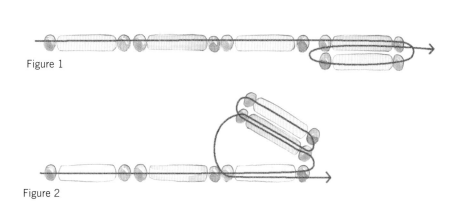

Figure 1

Figure 2

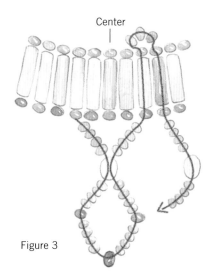

Center

Figure 3

Figure 4

Figure 5

to the center of the bottom of the circle. Begin a new thread that exits two segments away from the center. String 4C, 1 pearl, 4C, 1B, 4C, 1A, 4C, 1B, and 4C. Pass back through the pearl. String 4C, skip three ladder segments, pass up through the next segment, exiting at the neck side of the ladder. String 3C and pass down through the next segment to make a picot. String 4C, 1 pearl, and 4C. Pass through the nearest B from the previous netted section (Figure 3).

Continue making netting and picots until you reach the end of the ladder.

Position a soldered jump ring so that half is hidden behind the edge of the first

bead segment. Pass the needle through the jump ring and back through the segment several times until the jump ring is secure. Secure the thread and trim.

Finish the second half of the necklace with netting and picots. Secure the second soldered jump ring to the other end of the ladder. When the ladder is completely netted, place a pin at the bottom point of each netted section.

JOINING LADDERS
Make a second ladder in the same way you did the first. This ladder should be long enough to extend from the first netted point to the last. Using the netted points as a guide, pin the second

ladder securely around the free end of the netting. Next, make a third ladder and pin it around the second ladder so that the edges are aligned.

Start a new thread on the second ladder that exits on the inner edge of the first segment. Pass through the A bead at the point of the first section of netting and back through the second segment of both the second and third ladders. Continue connecting the ladders to the netting (Figure 4). After you have woven through several sets of segments, the two ladders will no longer line up correctly, so every so often, skip a segment on the outermost ladder.

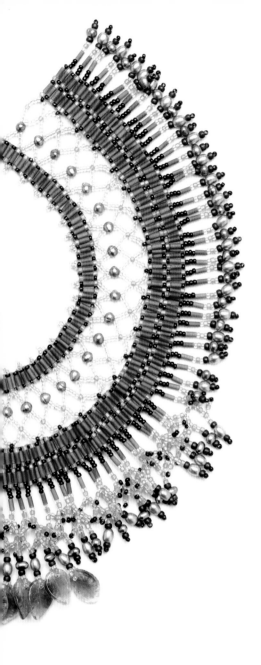

FRINGE

Make fringe on the outside of the collar. I used simple fringe (Figure 5) to embellish the first third and last third of the necklace, and two variations of branch fringe for the remaining (central) third (Figures 6 and 7). When you work the fringe, simply exit from a bead on the outside of the third ladder, string the beads required for the fringe leg, skip the last bead strung (or beads, depending on the type of fringe used), and pass back through the rest.

Pass up through the next bead on the ladder and down through the following bead.

When the fringe is complete, use unsoldered jump rings to attach the clasp to the soldered jump rings stitched to each end of the necklace.

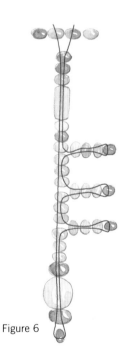

Figure 6

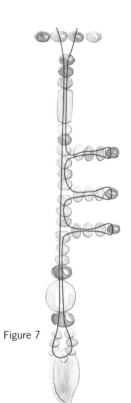

Figure 7

PINTO BEAR NECKLACE

Mary Hicklin

"From earliest times, fetishes have been used as messengers to assist in communications with spirits and deities. The Zuni (Ashiwi) people carve beautiful fetishes from stone, shell, antler, wood, and other natural materials. Today most commercially available fetishes are better described as 'carvings,' art objects that have not been ceremonially blessed—but they are alive with the power of the stones from which they were carved, the animals in whose shape they were made, and the energy of their makers.

"One does not have to be a shaman to pray that a blessing go along with the gift of a lovely carving. Wearing a fetish necklace can be merely a fashion statement, a reminder to be mindful, or a totem for protection, healing, or other types of help the power animal brings.

"I work with these living symbols with enormous respect and care, choosing only those that speak to me and waiting for the individual piece to show me how it wants to be embellished. The bear fetish for this necklace was carved by Zuni carvers Peter and Dinah Gasper out of turquoise from the Number 8 mine in northern Nevada. The bear belongs to the group of protective and healing animals in Zuni tradition. He is the protective animal of the direction west and is associated with strength and introspection. The color of the west in Zuni tradition is blue. A carving whose color is the same as the color of the animal's direction is especially powerful. Because the bear resembles man in its ability to stand, it is thought to be open to communication with man and is seen as a mediator between humans and spirits.

"As a hiker who has encountered Bear, I see why Bear is given the attribute of strength. His power is awesome. Bear demonstrates his superior intelligence by raiding virtually any food cache a backpacker can devise, and the she-bear's fierce protection of cubs is legendary. Cubs are born during semihibernation and remind us of the importance of making quiet time for ourselves. I have also seen how Bear loves salmon, which represents wisdom in Celtic tradition. In the fall, Bear paves the Rogue River Trail with salmon skins.

"The bear is an animal of the moon and the goddess Diana, so he is linked to the unconscious. The bear's hibernation cave is likened to the place of inner knowing, the dream lodge at the center of the four lobes of the brain—the third eye and the cave of Brahma. Rather than engage in roof-brain activity, however, try Bear's own strategy: quiet the mind, enter the dream lodge, and allow Bear to speak."

MATERIALS

Carved fetish, with or without a medicine bundle

Assorted coordinating stone, glass, and silver beads

Coordinating heishi

Assorted charms, crystals, seed beads, and smaller stone beads (for tassel)

Sterling necklace cones

Crimp beads

4" of 16-gauge sterling wire or purchased hook closure (all wire should be dead soft)

8" of 18-gauge sterling wire (or enough to attach necklace cones)

4" of 18-gauge sterling wire for each segment of the extension (you may need smaller-gauge wire to fit through the beads or you may have to drill the beads to accept the wire)

6" of 18-gauge sterling wire (or enough to attach the fetish to the necklace)

6" of 22-gauge sterling wire (or enough to wrap the fetish and attach the tassel)

Medium or heavy beading wire, depending on weight of beads and fetish

Nymo D thread

Beeswax

GS Hypo Cement or knot burner

Tiny seashell, blue cornmeal, and crushed turquoise or pollen (optional)

TOOLS

Smooth-jawed chain-nose pliers

Round-nose pliers

Flush cutter

Small #3 or #5 jeweler's file

Cable nippers

Crimping pliers

Beading needle, sized for seed beads used

Scissors

Thimble

Safety glasses

TECHNIQUES

Stringing (page 156)

Crimping (page 156)

Wirework (page 153)

Tubular peyote stitch (page 153)

Fringes (page 154)

Knots (page 151)

MAKING THE TASSEL

Begin making the tassel by preparing your carving. A fetish often has an offering bundle wrapped around it with sinew or imitation sinew. The bundle empowers the fetish. The carver may or may not have intended for the fetish to be suspended from this wrap. You may have to provide a coordinating wrap with sufficient strength to support the piece.

If your carving does not have an offering bundle, you may wish to make one with sinew or imitation sinew, an arrowhead, and a few tiny beads of turquoise, coral, shell, or other material. Wrap the arrowhead first, then make a separate wrap for the beads. Tie the bundle with a simple unobtrusive square knot or with larger decorative knots on either side of the bundle.

Thread 22-gauge silver wire through the wrap so the sinew doesn't stretch and wear. You will be using this wrap as an attachment point to the larger necklace.

Figure 1

Cut 6" of 18-gauge wire and make a wrapped loop that captures the sinew/wire attachment point above the arrowhead. String 1 spacer, 1 rondelle, 1 barrel, 1 nugget, 1 barrel, 1 rondelle, and 1 spacer. Make another wrapped loop to secure the beads (Figure 1).

Next add the tassel under the fetish. Cut 6" of 22-gauge wire and make a small wrapped loop at one end. String enough heishi to wrap around the fetish. Position the loop under the fetish and wrap the fetish securely. For my carving, I used the offering bundle to ensure the wrap didn't fall off. Each fetish presents a unique challenge—sometimes wrapping near the offering bundle works, but sometimes you'll need to wrap a narrow point on the body. Wrap the open wire end in the opposite direction from the original wrap so the ends meet nicely (Figure 2). Trim and file smooth.

Make the tassel under the fetish by using needle and thread to make fringe off the loop just created. Glue the knots. Cover the wire loop with seed beads using tubular peyote stitch. Start at the top and increase to make a bell shape.

Figure 2

STRINGING

Cut two 4" pieces of 18-gauge wire and make a small wrapped loop at one end of each wire. Make sure the loop fits well when you string it onto a cone. It's okay to smush the wrap a bit to fit—it won't show.

Figure 3

Figure 4

Figure 5

Attach 25" of beading wire to one of the loops. Secure it with one or two crimp beads. Test the crimps to be sure they hold. String 1 cone from the inside out so the wire loop is hidden inside it (Figure 3). Make a wrapped loop on the silver wire extending from the cone. Make sure the wrap sits right against the cone to secure the strung portion of the necklace. String 1 nugget, 1 spacer, 1 nugget, 1 spacer, 1 nugget, 1 silver bead, 1 rondelle, 1 silver bead four times. String 1 nugget, 1 spacer, and the tassel.

String the other side of the necklace in reverse order. Before attaching the beading wire to the second silver wire loop, examine your work carefully to be sure the beads are correctly ordered, the fetish hangs in the middle, and the length is appropriate. Make any necessary adjustments. Snug all the beads and crimp to the second wire loop. Trim the beading wire. String the second cone and make a wrapped loop as you did before, but this time capture within the loop the hook side of the clasp (Figure 4).

MAKING THE CHAIN LINK

The chain-link extension allows the necklace to be worn at various longer lengths.

Cut 4" of 18-gauge wire. Make a wrapped loop large enough for the clasp hook to fit through. Hammer the loop gently just above the cross in the wire. Capture the wrapped loop on the eye portion (not the hook side) of the clasp. Make the wrap, trim, and file smooth. String 1 nugget, make a wrapped loop to secure the bead, and gently hammer the loop (Figure 5). Repeat this step four times, each time attaching the new loop to the previous link.

FEEDING THE FETISH

Feed your fetish blue cornmeal, crushed turquoise, or pollen, served in a tiny seashell.

PERUVIAN CAT TOTEM BAG

Susan Guagliumi

"In the late sixties, I purchased a revision of *Textiles of Ancient Peru and Their Techniques* by Raoul d'Harcourt, a wonderful book first published in 1934 with black-and-white detail photos of the *Paracas Mantle*. This ceremonial cloth, found in a pre-Inca tomb on the peninsula of Paracas, is an ancient piece of plain-weave, warp-wrapped cloth that is a mere 49 by 19¼" (124.5 by 49 cm), bordered by ninety small figures. These figures, worked in wool with loop-stitch embroidery over canvas tapes, depict a pantheon of intertwined animal, human, and plant forms—and although there are many theories, nobody really knows what they symbolize. I was hooked by their mystery and intricacy, and Peruvian textiles came to represent for me (as for many textile junkies) the ultimate standard against which all other textiles are judged.

"In January 2002, a friend asked me to accompany her to a colleague's wedding in Peru. The bride's brother-in-law knew the curator at the anthropology museum in Lima and arranged a private visit to the archives while the museum was closed to the public. I was grateful for my rudimentary Spanish when the curator asked '*Que quieres ver?*' ('What would you like to see?'). My eyes filled with tears as she rolled open drawer after drawer of Paracas embroideries, tapestries, knotted and looped and netted pieces, gauze weaves, and intensely colored feather capes. Later, my friend and I each confessed to using the excuse of straightening a fringe or plucking off a hair to actually touch those incredible relics. That week we also visited Cuzco and Machu Picchu, which was as close to a religious experience as I have come in a very long time. I left Peru at the end of the week feeling renewed and inspired.

"The amulet purse *Ancient Cat Out of the Bag*—featuring a motif from plate 29 of the d'Harcourt book—is fringed with Mexican milagro arms and eyes as a votive offering for my craft. I want to be sure that I enter my old age with acuity and strength. The work of my hands has provided me with some of my most satisfying moments, and I cannot bear the thought of growing old and being unable to work. A common motif in Peruvian art and textiles, the cat represents a feline deity. For this piece, I worked on mesh screening as a nod to the ancient gauze fabrics the Peruvians produced."

Aluminum window screening 13 × 7" (33 × 18 cm) for a finished bag measuring 5½ × 6" (14 × 15 cm)

Size 15° seed beads in assorted colors

Silamide thread

G-S Hypo Cement

¾–1" (2–2.5 cm) wide Ultrasuede, for strap of desired length

Milagros

Masking tape

TOOLS

Size 13 beading needles

Scissors

Smooth metal thimble

Sewing machine

TECHNIQUES

Fringes (page 154)

This bag is worked with seed beads on common aluminum window screening, much the same way that beads are woven on a loom. Copper and brass screening work well, too, but they are more rigid and do not allow the beads to ease into place quite as easily, so experiment first with the softer aluminum screening. The darker screen also offers a great contrast to the beads and creates dramatic color effects and texture.

MAKING THE BAG

Cut the screening a bit larger than the finished project in case some edge wires loosen. I usually tape all four edges with masking tape to prevent loosening—and to keep the threads from getting caught on the wire ends as I work.

I threaded the appropriate number and color of beads for a single row onto the needle from the back of the work. Then I pushed one bead into each space within the mesh. I poked the needle through to the front of the screening and then passed it back through each of the beads to anchor the row in the mesh. You really have to pop the beads through the mesh—they are a snug fit—and you

also have to make sure they stay put as you pass the needle back through them. (I sometimes used a smooth metal thimble to protect my nails.) Large, solid areas of beads can be difficult to work because the screen tightens on itself, so avoid dense designs when you use this technique.

When you're finished with the beading, secure all threads within the work and glue all the knots.

To make the bag, I folded the screening to size and basted the edges together. I cut a length of Ultrasuede to make a strap and bound the edges of the bag by

folding the strap around them. I chose Ultrasuede because I like its texture and workability—and the fact that it doesn't have to be hemmed. To my delight, the sewing machine sailed smoothly through the bound screen edges! I finished the bag with fringes worked with two colors of seed beads and Mexican milagros.

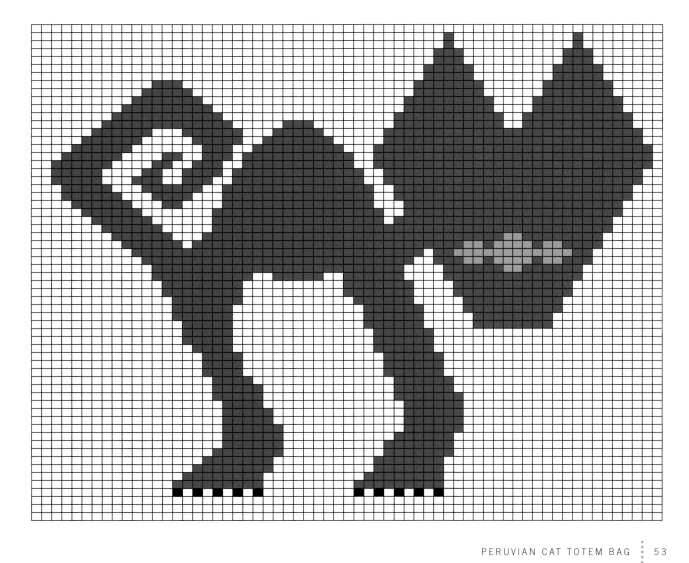

ARMILLARY AND COSMIC ORBIT

Victoria Hughes

"I made *Armillary* during a very challenging time in my life, when I was considering suicide as a choice for relieving pain. Creating this necklace was about exploring and illustrating what kept me here, how the universe operated, where my place was within it, and what quality—so deep down inside me that I couldn't even identify it in that moment—kept me from leaving a life that I felt was full of grief and betrayal.

"From the time of the ancient Greeks through the Renaissance, scientists viewed the universe as a reflection of Divine Order. Science was a verification of the divine, not a negation of it. Theoretical models wove together beauty, magic, and the most up-to-date scientific data available.

"An armillary is an early model of the Earth, Sun, stars, and planets. Narrow rings circle around a central body to portray the relationships of celestial circles—the bands of the heavens, the Earth's or Sun's ecliptic, the zodiac, and the orbits of comets—to each other and to the central point.

"At the time I made *Armillary* these ideas about the universe were close to my own—great wheels of purpose and awareness, arcs of time and space, with me somewhere within it all. I felt my identity was an aspect of the universe, within the universe, moving within the influences of various larger circles of power, destiny, and inevitable, endless growth—like a shining ball in a Rube Goldberg machine, going where gravity or some other compulsive force inexorably pulled me. I wanted to know those forces well enough that I could understand them, maybe accept them, and eventually work with them instead of feeling manipulated, bereft of power, and resistant.

"In this circular, sculptural neckpiece, the wearer is at the center of 'influences' that move, stately and constant, around her. Zodiac symbols are inscribed on one narrow band, the planets on another. The progression of numbers known as the Fibonacci series—whose spiraling expansion defines the Golden Mean, a mathematical constant that governs relationships and growth patterns within nature and throughout the cosmos—is inscribed on a third band. Some elements arch slightly away from the body, and the

WORKING FROM WITHIN

Each of us has philosophical "magnets," specific questions that we are drawn to again and again throughout our lives. These questions are an ongoing conversation that our day-to-day self has with the larger, inner self that we truly are.

How do we move from these questions, complex ideas, and feelings to create a finished piece? I have developed five steps to help you begin to channel your energy and explore the creative process on a level deep enough to create a piece that is personally meaningful and satisfying.

SET YOUR INTENTION

Why do want to make the piece? What do you hope to accomplish with this creative gesture? I am not asking you what the object is. I am asking why you want to make it. When you know your intention, it's easy to calmly select and work with the best materials. A lack of a clear

imagery continues around to the back to the clasp as an integral part of the design. The steel mainspring of an antique pocket watch, various brass gears, small planets, and other elements are references to the machinery of the cosmos and time and space.

"My awareness of myself and of the processes of the universe has changed much in the twelve years since I made *Armillary*. So much water has gone under the bridge that the bridge is gone. I'm living a new lifetime—and even have taken to using my full first name instead of the name Tory that I was known by then. More and more, I understand the great gift of change and transformation inherent in a situation that forces resolution. *Cosmic Orbit* (left), made in 2005, is the counterpoint to *Armillary*. While I was making it, I asked the same questions but found new answers.

"*Cosmic Orbit* reflects a calm, simple sense of self and spirit. In *Armillary*, the cosmic orbit was around and outside of me. Now I am within it, and it is within me. The golden line is an opening spiral, rather than a closed circle. I accept the rhythm and grace of the organic cycles in which we move and the constant unity of divine and human awareness, which flows around and through all of us. All is one, expressing and expanding."

purpose or intention can knot up your creative flow and be paralyzing.

For instance, your intention may be "to experiment with new materials" or "to make a present for my sister" or "to create a sculpture illustrating my spiritual beliefs." Or it may be "to goof around to see what happens, which might also relieve this tension headache"—all intentions are valid.

Choose one and follow it with conviction and vitality. There are no wrong

answers, nothing to judge, just choices to make.

START WITH WHAT WORKS

Ask questions about what works for you emotionally and conceptually. What excites you? What do you really love? If you could experience anything, what would it be? What are your delights and passions? What are your deep, simple truths? Make a poem about these things, or a song, or a list on a favorite type of paper.

Let go of others' definitions and assumptions. Everyone's creative process is different. Yours is exquisitely tuned to support your own creative gifts. Give yourself the things that work for you, and you're already on the path to greater creative response. You will begin to reintegrate yourself into your life and actions.

ALLOW YOURSELF TO EXPERIMENT

The creative process continually opens up possibilities. When something unexpected happens, or a tempting detour whispers to you, don't judge it as a mistake. Instead look closely at it, listen to its message, and see how you can incorporate it into your work. If something suggests itself to you while you are midstream, try it. Then decide how or whether to use it.

If you decide that you already know the only and best route to your destination, you are going to be frustrated when you encounter obstacles—and you might also miss an exciting opportunity. Court the unexpected, follow up on that mischievous, impish concept, or that new technical idea that's been teasing you. Observe where it leads you.

TAKE CARE OF YOUR TOOLS

When we think of tools, we think of pliers, scissors, and X-acto knives, but those are just the little tools. The big tools are body, mind, and spirit—and they need more care and maintenance than the others. The little tools can easily be replaced. The big tools provide the channel through which all of your creative energy moves.

Although blocks and fears can temporarily obstruct that channel, you are naturally designed for free-flowing energy. Whenever things don't feel easy and active, there are adjustments to be made. Never confuse the block with who you are.

Being creative requires all of you, your whole self. A successful, fulfilling creative life will flourish only if your whole self is flourishing. Sometimes when it's hard to make things, it's because one of your big tools needs some attention.

If you feel blocked, check in with yourself. Ask yourself what makes you feel happy and well. Have you been getting enough fresh air? Have you spent some time with yourself? Are you sleeping well? Have you taken the opportunity to do something you love—like dance or play Frisbee? Move more, watch less TV. Keep your own channel coming in with the best reception. Strong, person-

ally satisfying creativity flows most easily through a healthy system.

ACT ON YOUR INTUITION

Listen to your intuition, trust it, and—most important—act on it. Creativity is a web that extends throughout our conscious and unconscious awareness. The way we access this web—in order to be as creative as we'd like to be in any moment—is by listening to our own inner voice. Your intuition is another big tool. Respect it and act on the information it gives you. By trusting your intuition, you cultivate it and increase your ability to hear it often. Act on it as soon as it presents itself and you will maintain a steady flow.

Do you realize what you're really doing when you make something? All aspects of yourself come together in these magnificent moments when you move stuff around, do a little of this, a little of that. You are creating something that does not exist anywhere in the universe until you—you!—make it. You transform the pure energy of your idea into a physical form. The communication that flows through you—linking the idea and the form—is the essence of creativity. And creativity is a spiritual act.

Text adapted from *Polymer: The Chameleon Clay*, 2002, with permission from Krause Publications.

chapter four

BEADING FOR GOOD

Whether to celebrate a happy event, invite an auspicious beginning, or simply summon the best of human nature—in yourself or others—there is reason to bead. In various traditions, beads and stones have stood alone as talismans of virtue and wisdom. They have also embellished the amulets, ornaments, and costumes featured in rituals to ensure bountiful harvests and fortunate marriages and to welcome the birth of children.

Children are important in every society. They will continue the culture and shape its future character. So, as newborns arrive, the family and community greet them and wish them well and, with respect and gratitude, acknowledge the ancestral thread they extend.

Among Native American people—from the Subarctic to the Plains—new mothers traditionally made amulets to guard and guide the lives of their children. When the infant lost the umbilical cord, the mother would enclose it in a buckskin pouch, which she decorated with beadwork. She would hang

The umndwana *dolls of the Ndebele of South Africa wear beaded rings similar to the arm and leg bracelets worn by young women during their initiation ceremonies. The doll is a symbol of the woman's next phase of life, during which she will bear children. From the collection of Jeanne Criscola.*

the pouch around the baby's neck or attach it to the cradle to ensure that the baby have a long and healthy life. The pouch had the shape of an animal whose traits the mother hoped the child would share and whose spirit would be a lifelong companion.

After a child's birth, the Xhosa of South Africa hold a ceremony to ask for the blessings of the ancestors. The father gives each of the guests—members of the extended family—two small white beads as he expresses his wish for the baby's health and prosperity. (White is the color of purity, and only white beads are offered to the spirits.) The guests ask for blessings as they return the beads, which the mother strings into a necklace. She then places the necklace around the infant's neck before presenting the newest family member to the others.

In many African cultures, beads mark each significant phase of life from infancy through adulthood. Young men and women wear elaborate beadwork to mark their coming of marriageable age. Beaded garments and jewelry are designed to catch the eyes of potential suitors during initiation ceremonies—at which the young people are introduced into society as adults. These rituals mark the beginning of the courtship period, which eventually leads to marriage.

Many young women make beaded dolls to express their desire and readiness for children. These dolls are often featured in initiation ceremonies. A Tsonga doll, which is called a *nwana* ("child"), wears a skirt resembling those worn by adult women. In some cultures, a man may give his fiancée a beaded doll of the same gender as the child he hopes she will bear.

In China, as a young girl comes of age, she receives a piece of jade. The ideal gift for a man to give his intended is a jade butterfly. Jade is considered the essence of love, and the butterfly is the Chinese symbol for the soul. A young couple may receive a jade carving of a man riding a unicorn to symbolize the hope that they will have a male child.

The Chinese have worn jade—in one of its two forms, nephrite and jadeite—for thousands of years. The Chinese believe jade is of supernatural origin, associated with dragons, celestial beings of good fortune. Jade is a symbol of long life, sound health, and prosperity. Many Chinese carry the stone with them and frequently take it in hand hoping to benefit from direct contact. The ancient philosopher Confucius believed jade embodied all the qualities that define excellence and virtue. An ancient Chinese ideograph for "king" is drawn as three strung jade beads.

Pearls are also auspicious symbols. Chinese dragon gods are often depicted with a flaming pearl, a symbol of spiritual perfection. In Hindu writings, the pearl is associated with the god Krishna, who plucked one from the sea to present to his daughter as a wedding gift. The Romans and Greeks associated the pearl with Venus and Aphrodite, their respective goddesses of love and beauty. Pearls symbolize the Moon, purity, and fertility, and, according to the legends of the pearl divers of Borneo, they can actually reproduce themselves.

Because of their rarity and desirability, jade and pearl have also always had great monetary value. Wearing them not only ensures good fortune but also displays it. Likewise, many people have strung coins into jewelry as amulets for good fortune and symbols of prosperity. Women in the West African savannah wear silver coins in their hair to indicate their families' wealth. Berber women traditionally wore jewelry made from French, Spanish, and Swiss coins—traces of conquering cultures turned to decorative ends.

Each of us strives for what is good in life, although each may define the concept differently. Some hope for material well-being—prosperity, security, an easy path. Others strive for spiritual well-being—the full expression of our best nature. As the work of the designers in this chapter suggests, the wisest of us aspire to both.

In China, jade is a symbol of virtue and status. This carved Chinese nephrite disk combines the traditional motifs of dragon and cloud. In Chinese, Korean, and Japanese, the characters for "jade" and "bead" are the same within the language. Jade was also valued by the ancient Mayans and Aztecs and the people of New Zealand and the Middle East. Collection of The Field Museum, object #1689.183343, A101880c.

The traditional Spanish-influenced necklaces of Guatemala, called chachales, *often contain coral or red beads and silver Spanish, Mexican, and South American coins. Some antique* chachales *also contain "pieces of eight," old Spanish pesos, which Guatemalans believed would bring good luck when the necklaces were received as gifts.* From the collection of Lee Price Arellano. Photo by Robert K. Liu, Ornament.

CHINESE GOOD FORTUNE POUCH

Helen Banes

"In 1986, I had the good fortune to accompany my husband during his assignment from the Chinese government to advise its scientists on methods of drug analysis. As an official guest, I was offered the opportunity to visit a silk factory and jade and jewelry facilities.

"When it was time for us to leave, as a parting gesture of appreciation, my husband and I arranged a dinner party at our hotel. As we prepared to pay the bill—which had been calculated by abacus—we learned that the hotel did not accept credit cards. Upon hearing this news, we had to divest ourselves of most of our traveler's checks, which we had intended to use on the remaining portion of the trip.

"Since that experience, China has become a successful world marketplace. *Chinese Good Fortune Pouch* is my tribute not only to the good friends we made while we were in China but to the resilience of the Chinese people.

"In Chinese culture, coins have long been used as amulets. Silver coins ensure prosperity and long life, and symbolize the divine mountains of the south. I also added a silver cloud pin to the pouch. The cloud represents good fortune, happiness, and prosperity, and it correlates to the principles of yin and yang, the forces that create change in the universe. This functional pouch is suitable for carrying money—and is just the right size to hold a credit card."

MATERIALS

5mm round glass beads in blue, turquoise, and coral

5mm sterling silver plain spacer beads

7 Chinese coins with one small hole at the top and two at the bottom

2½ × 3½" (6.5 × 9 cm) piece of Ultrasuede or other sturdy fabric backing

Spool of 18-gauge 2- or 3-ply waxed carpet linen (for warp)

2 or 3 colors of pearl cotton #3 (for weft)

Spool of 8-lb monofilament

Decorative pin (optional)

Clear-drying glue

5 × 8" (12.5 × 20.5 cm) thick foam-core, 2 pieces stacked and taped together

TOOLS

Size 14 beading pins

Size 18 and 20 tapestry needles

Small metal or wooden fork

Small scissors

TECHNIQUES

Knots (page 151)

Fringes (page 154)

Braiding (page 156)

CREATING THE BEADED WARP

Tape a copy of Figure 1 to the foamcore. Firmly insert pins where shown along the top and bottom edges of the design. Insert the pins at a 45° angle so that the pinheads face away from the design.

Anchor the warp thread to the pin marked A with a slipknot, allowing a 3" (7.5 cm) tail. Holding the thread taut, alternately wrap the warp over the top and bottom pins. End the thread at the pin marked B with another slipknot, leaving a 3" (7.5 cm) tail (Figure 1).

Remove the bottom pin (Row 1). Cut a 3"(7.5 cm) length of monofilament and insert it between the warp threads you just released. Bend the monofilament so its ends meet to create a beading needle. Push each bead onto the monofilaments and then up the threads (Figure 2). Follow Figure 1 to determine where to position the beads. Continue to bead the row, replacing the pin at the bottom of the beads to secure them and to keep the warp threads taut. Repeat the process with the remaining rows to bead the body of the pouch. Then repeat the process to create the beaded fringe on the lower edges of the warp.

Remove the bottom pin of Row 1 again and work with the monofilament to attach a coin to the warp with a lark's head knot (Figure 3). Insert the pin into the opening of the coin to secure the beads and hold the warp in tension. Repeat to add coins to the ends of the remaining warp threads.

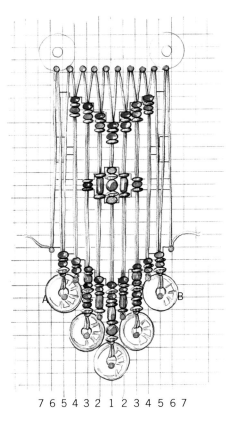

7 6 5 4 3 2 1 2 3 4 5 6 7

Figure 1

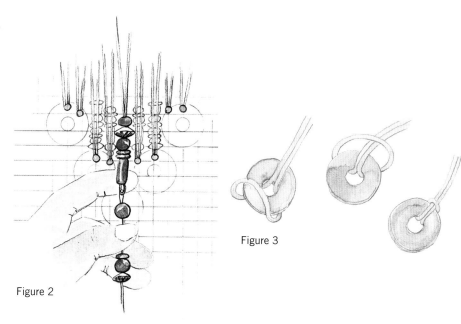

Figure 2

Figure 3

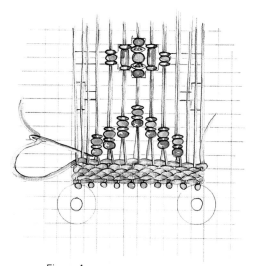

Figure 4

Illustrations based on techniques from *Fiber & Bead Jewelry; Beautiful Designs to Make & Wear* by Helen Banes with Sally Banes, © 2000 by Helen Banes. A Sterling/Chapelle book, published by Sterling Publishing Co., New York.

WEAVING

To begin weaving, turn the foamcore so the top edge of the design faces toward you. Thread the needle with a 30" (76 cm) length of pearl cotton.

Lay the tail ends of the warp thread along the outer edges of the warp. As you weave, weave around the ends to join them to the warp and conceal them—this way, you won't need to make knots.

Begin weaving under the first outer warp thread at the right edge, then over the next warp thread. Be sure to weave each individual thread in the warp pair separately. Continue under and over across the entire width. When you finish the row, pack the weft tightly by gently beating the warp. Do so by pushing the just-woven weft threads toward the pins with the fork to tighten the weaving.

To begin the next row, reverse the process, working in the opposite direction. Weave under the warp threads you wove over in the previous row (Figure 4). In each row that has a bead, weave up to the bead, then reverse direction. Beat the warp each time you weave a row. Every two rows will create a solid line of color.

CHANGING COLORS OR STARTING A THREAD

When you are ready to change colors—or need to begin a new thread—weave the end of the old thread back through four rows of weaving by passing the needle up along a warp thread at the back of the weaving to conceal the end.

Thread the needle with the new thread and conceal the end the same way, passing the needle in the opposite direction along the warp thread. You can start or end a thread at any point in the piece. Continue weaving in pattern.

When you reach one of the slipknots (A, B), pass the weaving thread through the loop of the knot at least twice. This wrap will secure the warp threads at the edge of the piece to the body.

COMPLETING THE BODY

Turn the foamcore again so that the bottom of the design faces you. Warp ends that have coin dangles do not require further finishing. To secure the ends that have beads, remove the pin that is holding the beads in place. Insert a small length of warp thread—about 2" (5 cm)—through the loop in the end of the warp pair. Knot the added thread. Apply a drop of glue to the knot before trimming.

CREATING THE POUCH AND STRAP

If desired, attach a decorative pin after you've woven the piece. Remove all the top and bottom pins in the foamcore. Attach the Ultrasuede or fabric to the back of the woven piece to form a pouch, handstitching along the two sides and the bottom.

Stitch the remaining two coins to the outer top edges of the weaving with a length of the same thread you used for the warp.

To make each strap, fold three 36" (91.5 cm) lengths of weft thread in half—work with threads that are the same color as those in the weaving. Loop the folded end through one coin at the top edge and secure with a lark's head knot. Braid the strands and knot the end. The two straps tie around the neck, so the necklace length can be adjusted.

TWO FETISH BAGS

David Dean

"Umbilical cord fetish bags have long been a fascination of mine. When a child is born to a Native American family, the child is lavished with the most spiritual and elaborately decorated clothing and baby objects. Fully beaded cradleboards, bonnets, and umbilical cord bags were—and are—a way of honoring the lives of the mother and child. The maker of the fetish bag is also honored by building this very special decoration for the baby.

"In building a fetish bag, it is important that the maker give thanks for the child and pray for the baby's health and welfare. If a fetish bag is so blessed, it will serve as a long and faithful good luck omen for the child. The maker must understand that this gift will stay with the child for life and will serve as a reminder of the traditional ways of the parents.

"Traditionally, a new mother or close female relative made this type of bag when a child was born. When the baby's umbilical cord fell off, the cord was put into the bag. The bag was also stuffed with buffalo wool, sage, sweetgrass, or flat cedar—depending on the maker and the tribe.

"In some tribes, girls are still given turtle-shaped bags, and boys receive bags in the shapes of lizards or snakes. The maker hopes that the child will have the attributes of that animal. Turtles are known for their long life spans, lizards and snakes for their stealth and speed. The legends, purpose, and use of the bag vary depending on the beliefs of the tribe of origin.

"The umbilical cord fetish bag is often hung on the outside of the cradleboard as a good luck charm and as a decoration to entertain the child. In some tribes, after the child begins to walk, the bag is attached to the child's belt. In others, the umbilical cord fetish bag becomes a part of that person's medicine bundle. Or the bag becomes one of the mother's possessions, serving as a sort of 'birth certificate' for the child."

Cut two identical turtle or lizard shapes from the buckskin or leather (Figures 1 and 2). Place the two pieces together and whipstitch the edges with a beading needle and Nymo D thread, but leave one side open. Turn the bag inside out so that the stitches are on the inside. Stuff the bag as much as possible with the sweetgrass, buffalo wool, or batting. Whipstitch the open side together with the remaining thread.

The beadwork is done next, typically with lane stitch. Because the bags are so small, keep the designs very simple, using only three to five colors.

Add the animal's legs. For the turtle, cut four pieces of buckskin $2 \times \frac{3}{4}"$ (5×2 cm) and trim each strip as in Figure 3 to create fringe. Roll each strip lengthwise and whipstitch to close (Figure 4).

Stitch each leg in position and bead a simple design around it. For the lizard, cut four $3 \times \frac{1}{4}"$ (7.5×6 mm) buckskin strips. Add tin cones to the ends of each strip, fold the strips in half, and sew them to the body. If desired, sew a length of leather lacing to the head and tie the ends to hang the fetish.

MATERIALS

For each fetish bag

Size 13° seed beads in a variety of colors

$1–1\frac{1}{4}"$ tin cones

Two $5 \times 5"$ pieces of soft buckskin or other soft leather

Buckskin thong, $\frac{1}{4}"$ wide

2 oz sweetgrass, buffalo wool, or cotton batting

Nymo D thread

Leather lacing (optional)

TOOLS

Beading needle

Scissors

TECHNIQUES

Lane stitch (page 155)

Whipstitch (page 155)

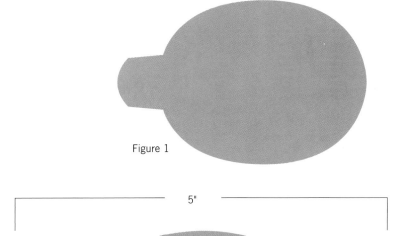

3½"

Figure 1

5"

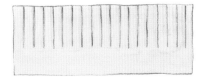

Figure 2

Figure 3

Figure 4

PEARL PEACE DOVE NECKLACE

Isis Ray

"I'm inspired by the art of native, indigenous people who live close to the earth and recognize the magic in nature. Beads are a way for people to connect to that magic and to create an atmosphere for contemplation, to slow down in a fast-paced world and touch something made by hand, evoking the spirit. I was raised as a theosophist and a third-generation vegetarian. My mother was an amazing person who taught my brother and me to respect all people, all cultures, all religions, and all forms of life as equal in importance, and to recognize the interconnectedness of all beings on Earth.

"Nature is my muse, and color and light are my means of expression, which is why I am drawn to the medium of glass beadmaking—to create objects that fully capture those qualities. I also believe in the healing powers of light and color, and I feel that it is more necessary than ever to create objects that promote peace and good will and generate a positive outlook on life. World peace is necessary for our planet to survive.

"The dove with an olive branch is a symbol of peace and of the renewal of life. Doves are sacred to many cultures and religions. They represent heavenly power and the life spirit or soul. To create the dove on this lampworked pendant, I used a technique I learned from painted-glass artist Cappy Thompson of Seattle, Washington. The method is similar to the one that artists used to create the medieval stained-glass windows of Europe. To make the pendant, I created a flat shape of clear glass and attached it to two beads in the torch flame. I painted the outline and the colored areas of the pendant with Reusche paints mixed with water and gum Arabic. I shaded the background area with a monochrome technique known as grisaille and fired the piece in the kiln three times—once after each stage of the painting.

"I strung the necklace with pearls, which—because they originate within the shell of an oyster—are a symbol of hidden knowledge and esoteric wisdom. They also symbolize patience and purity, birth and rebirth. The word 'pearl' in Italian (*perla*) is the word for 'bead,' and it is also my middle name."

MATERIALS

2" focal bead or pendant

½–¾" (1.3–2 cm) disk bead with 4mm hole

5mm pearls or other beads, 1 strand

Size 11° seed beads

2–3 sterling silver size 3–4mm spacer beads

2 sterling silver 5–6mm spacer beads with 2mm holes

1.9mm silver pendant slide

2 silver crimp beads

Medium beading wire

TOOLS

Wire cutters

Crimping pliers

Flat-nose pliers

TECHNIQUES

Stringing (page 156)

Crimping (page 156)

CONSIDERING COLOR AND DESIGN

I get inspiration for my color combinations from paintings, especially the work of the early-twentieth-century French painter Pierre Bonnard. He worked with a lot of complementary colors—shades of orange, violet, and green—and brought them to life by contrasting warm and cool colors. As you put colors together, remember that each one has to make the others better by its presence. The right combination makes the colors sing.

If I'm not sure about a design element in a strung piece, I try removing the element to see if the piece is better without it. Sometimes it's easier to tell what is wrong with a design—and simply remove those elements—than it is to know when the design is finished.

Balanced contrast is important, too, so create areas of dark and light throughout the design. Imagine the design in black and white with varying shades of gray. The patterns created by the different values should be balanced to create a design of their own. Areas of high contrast (black against white, for example) draw the viewer's eye, but if there is only one high-contrast area on the piece, the design will appear stagnant.

A symmetrical design—like the one for this necklace—is classic, elegant, and simple to create. Design one side of the piece and repeat the design as a mirror image on the other side. To add interest, place a dramatic focal-point bead at the center to draw the eye.

When I make an asymmetrical piece, I work with many types of beads of varying colors. Each bead has equal interest within the piece, and none overpowers any of the others. Unlike a symmetrical design, which has a central point of interest, an asymmetrical design has a lot of visual interest overall. The harmony of the design is created by the color combinations that dance around the piece, and the viewer's eye moves from one color relationship to the next. Just like patterns of contrast, the patterns of color should be balanced throughout the piece.

STRINGING THE NECKLACE

String all the beads for the necklace on the beading wire without cutting the wire off the spool.

When you have finished beading, make the end loop for the button-style closure. On one end of the wire, string one of the large spacer beads. Add the crimp bead and enough seed beads to form a loop that fits easily around the disk bead. Pass back through the crimp bead and crimp. Trim the end of the wire and slide the large spacer bead over the crimp to hide it.

Pull the other end of the beading wire so that all the beads are tight against the loop. Cut the wire about 5" (12.5 cm) from the last bead. Add another large spacer bead, 2 or 3 small spacer beads, a crimp bead, another small spacer bead, and the disk bead.

Pass through the loop in the pendant slide (the small jump ring attached to the silver tube). Pass back through the disk bead, the spacers, and the crimp bead. Pull the beads tight, using the flat-nose pliers and your thumbnail to slide the crimp bead as close as possible toward the other beads. Crimp and trim the wire.

Back of amulet shown here.

BEAD MOBILE

Beau Anderson

"Mobiles are abstract sculptures that harness the energy that comes to them and transform that energy into movement, colorful light, or sounds. Through an arrangement of thin forms, beads, rings, rods, or pieces of wood—balanced and suspended in midair—the energy is converted, and the mobile is set in motion. Mobiles change the space around them.

"This prayer mobile focuses on healing the critical balance on which the fine threads of all life hang. The framework is made of pieces of found driftwood and beaver chew, each from within functioning parts of different ecosystems. They represent the constant gifts of nature and how everything we do is balanced within nature.

"I started with these sticks and began to pray, bead by bead, to the basic elements that I asked for guidance. I am a flame worker and enjoy layering detailed images and energies into small areas to make the most of finite resources. As I made and strung each of these beads, I concentrated on inner peace and my hope for greater balance.

"Through evolution, we have overrun the planet and, in our race to consume, we have become less connected to Earth's delicate balance. Our unconsciousness leads to destruction, which over time has tipped the balance and now threatens the sacred strand of Earth's nature, the very fragile matrix of our unique gift of life.

"Mindful of the costs of overconsumption, I hope that people all over the world will choose to live more simply so that others can simply live. As the wind moves this piece, and as light illuminates it, I hope that people will realize the beauty of what we have.

"When I finished the piece, I held a small ceremony and, through meditation, infused the mobile with a prayer for balance: 'Balance is peace is happiness is joy is freedom is strength is protection.'"

MATERIALS

6–24" (15–61 cm) sticks or pieces of wood, 2 or more

Assorted glass beads

Assorted seed beads

Found objects

Heavyweight beading wire

Crimp beads

Lightweight fishing swivel

Ceiling hook or eye screw

TOOLS

Small knife

Crimping tool or pliers

Wire cutters

TECHNIQUES

Stringing (page 156)

Crimping (page 156)

PLANNING THE MOBILE

First decide where you want to hang the mobile. Well-lit areas with nearby movement or a slight breeze are ideal—an outside porch, a window, a chandelier, a tree. Make sure the wooden stud, support, or tree branch is strong enough to hold a piece of the finished size you are envisioning.

Measure the space in which the mobile will hang and write down the maximum dimensions. Imagine how you want the mobile to make you feel, how you want it to make the space feel—balanced, bold, reflective, peaceful, joyful, protected.

Go on a treasure hunt—your life is the map! Make a list of small objects that hold energy for you and gather them while focusing on the energies you want the mobile to emit. Choose beads of various shapes, sizes, and colors that you feel have those same energies.

CREATING THE MOBILE

Lay out the mobile by arranging the objects and beads in strands on a flat surface. Position them just as you want them to hang on the crosspieces. Be sure to plan at least one strand at each end of each crosspiece. The strands do not need to be the same length, but the length of the strands and the weight of the beads determine how the crosspieces will balance.

String large beads and found objects with smaller beads and seed beads. Consider each bead's relationship to the next so that you are telling a story as you create a strand. Make this process a

conscious ceremony by maintaining and refining the energy you wish to incorporate into each strand. Simply by being meditative as you work, you infuse that energy into the piece with each breath, touch, and thought.

Secure the bottom of the bead strands with crimp beads. For the top, string a crimp bead and then add enough seed beads to create a loop large enough to wrap around the crosspiece. Weave the wire end back through the crimp bead and crimp.

Before you make the top loop on the strand that will connect the two crosspieces, add the fishing swivel so that the arms of the mobile will swing freely. Make a beaded loop on the bottom end of the connecting strand.

Make another beaded loop at the top end of the strand that will hang from the wood support or branch—or add a small metal hook secured with a crimp bead.

On the bottom end of the remaining strands, add the crimp and seed beads and weave the loop through the hole of a large pendulous bead or found object. Loosely tie the bottom ends of each strand to secure the beads so you can test the balance of the mobile.

Loop the tops of the strands onto the crosspieces. Find the point of balance for each one by balancing the crosspiece on your fingers. The balancing point is determined by the amount of weight at each end and by the distribution of weight along the crosspiece. Play around with possibilities and adjust the strands as necessary by adding or removing beads.

Now join the two crosspieces with the connecting strand and hang the mobile to test and adjust its balance.

When you have found the arrangement you want, notch the wood with the knife so the beaded loops of the strands won't slide out of position and shift the balance. Remove the strands from the crosspieces. Untie the bottom ends, weave the wires back through the crimp

and seed beads, and secure the crimp bead. Then put the strands back on their crosspieces.

Hang the mobile as you create a ceremony that best embodies your intentions and sets them into motion.

chapter five

BEADING FOR PRAYER

To pray or meditate is to move attention away from mundane concerns into more ethereal realms. It is a way of communicating, either with a divine being or with the deepest aspects of your own nature. Prayers and meditations can be silent, spoken, or sung—or they can be strung, stitched, and arranged with beads.

The concept of prayer is laden with meaning, but, at its root, the word is linked to the bead. The Old English word for prayer is *bed*, the word *biddan* means "to pray or ask." The Sanskrit word for bead is related to the word for faith and the name of Buddha. The Spanish word for bead is *cuenta*, which also refers to counting—the function of beads in the prayer beads and rosaries that are part of many Eastern and Western traditions.

The number of beads in a prayer-bead strand has significant meaning within the belief system. The Roman Catholic rosary contains ten clusters of ten beads—each separated by one larger spacing bead—for each of the ten

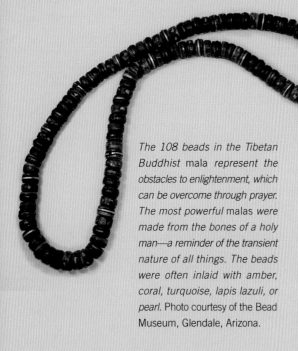

The 108 beads in the Tibetan Buddhist mala *represent the obstacles to enlightenment, which can be overcome through prayer. The most powerful* malas *were made from the bones of a holy man—a reminder of the transient nature of all things. The beads were often inlaid with amber, coral, turquoise, lapis lazuli, or pearl.* Photo courtesy of the Bead Museum, Glendale, Arizona.

"mysteries" in the life of Jesus. Muslims believe that Allah has ninety-nine known names and attributes, which they contemplate as they finger each of the ninety-nine beads in the prayer strand called a *subha* ("to praise").

Strands of beads are devices for remembering the sequence and number of prayers in a structured and significant cycle. Each bead is also a tactile aid to help the person praying to focus attention. The strands are held in one hand or two or pressed between the palms during prayer—but they are also worn around the neck or wrist as jewelry, as signs of faith, as marks of religious affiliation, and also as protective amulets.

The sensual pleasure of handling prayer beads has its own spiritual benefits—similar to the calming effect of the worry beads carried by men in Turkey, Greece, and the Middle East. The beads also serve as a physical reminder of the individual's connection to the divine and help instill a constantly prayerful state of mind.

In many cultures, people wear sacred writings for the same reason. In the Jewish tradition, men and boys about to be bar mitzvahed wear small black boxes called *tefillin*—one on the head and another on the arm—as physical reminders of their spiritual commitment. The boxes contain special parchment with handwritten verses from the Torah.

In Asia, the silver box called a *gau*—decorated with turquoise, coral, or other semiprecious stones—contains a handwritten Buddhist prayer blessed by a priest. In parts of Africa, people wear written verses from the Koran or incantations, known only to a holy man, in pendants of brass, copper, or silver (the metal of the prophet Mohammed). Native Americans carry sacred objects "given" to them in vision quests in small beaded pouches and medicine bags. These sacred amulets also offer protection to the wearer.

For the Huichol of Mexico, artwork itself is a form of prayer. Spiritual beliefs are encoded in embroidery, yarn paintings, and beadwork. For their sacred pilgrimage each year to "hunt" peyote, the Huichol create small beaded votive bowls called *rukuri*. The bowls are made from segments of gourds coated with beeswax. The makers press colored seed beads and symbolic objects into the warm wax and leave the bowls in sacred spots so the gods will drink the prayers within them.

As part of their religious ceremony, the Huichol eat peyote—a hallucinogenic cactus—which they believe puts them in contact with the gods. The gods then "give" the Huichol visions of intricate, sacred designs. In Huichol artwork, peyote is depicted as an eight-pointed star shape or as the toto flower. The motif, often found at the center of votive bowls and yarn paintings, serves as a powerful mandala, a means to enter the spirit world.

Mandalas also play an important role in the religious art and practices of Buddhist, Hindu, and Native American traditions. A mandala is a symmetrical, geometric design that represents the divine and physical worlds. At the center is the deity, sometimes in the form of a flower, wheel, or symbol. The word mandala is the Sanskirt word for circle—a powerful form in all cultures.

The mandala provides a focus for meditation and a gateway to enlightenment—the realization that the divine lies within one's self. Tibetan monks make intricate mandalas of jewels, stones, or colored sand. Each individual stone or granule is blessed, so the finished mandala has great energy. The mandala is then destroyed to symbolize the impermanence of life.

Prayer and meditation are traditional aspects of formal religions, with set precepts and significance, but ultimately they are very personal experiences. We pray for special intentions, or to express gratitude, reflect upon our lives, or connect with the spirit— within or beyond ourselves—that we rely on to guide us. With each bead, the prayer you make is your own.

The Huichol of Mexico create their votive bowls by pressing seed beads into warm beeswax. They sometimes add grains of corn, coins, and yarn to the design. Peyote is represented in Huichol artwork as an eight-pointed star or flower motif. The Huichol consider the peyote cacti the tracks of the sacred deer spirit, the intermediary between man and the gods. Photo courtesy of the American Museum of Natural History. *Reprinted by permission of the publisher from* The Art of the Huichol Indians, *Abrams, 1957.*

BEAD-EMBROIDERED ICON

Mary Walker

"This bead-embroidered icon, titled *Black Madonna*, is the first in a series of thirteen Mary pieces that I have made. The series is a way for me to reconnect with the feminine side of my faith tradition. Growing up Roman Catholic, I attended Mass six mornings a week during the school year at the Church of the Immaculate Conception. Sitting on the 'Mary side' of the church (as opposed to the 'Joseph side'), where the statue of Mary stood, I spent my childhood looking at the gem-colored images of this woman floating above me, suspended in the stained glass: Mary at the Annunciation, the Visitation, the Nativity, the Assumption—a strong, amazing figure gleaming in the sunlight. The visual power of these images made a far stronger impression on me than any of the traditional messages coming from the pulpit.

"My mother taught me to knit, and my grandmother taught me to embroider. One summer I was given an 'Indian' beading loom. The only source of beads in our small town was the Woolworth's dime store, but that was enough to keep me busy. After my second daughter was born, I took a watercolor class at a Benedictine retreat center. My wonderful teacher, Barbara DeVault, reinforced what I'd always known, if never completely articulated: Artwork is sacred work. I would go so far as to say that all work—anything done well—is sacred work. In this class, I finally combined my love of embroidery, beadwork, and watercolor. The first time I sewed beads into one of my paintings the flow of grace was unmistakable.

"As a child, I fingered my rosary beads as I prayed—and as an adult, I still do. The beads in my art are simply another type of prayer bead, just as sacred and, for me, even more meaningful. The light reflected and scattered by the beads resembles all the magnificent, sacred, stained-glass images found throughout the world. The circular shape of the round beads echoes the sacred circle of life, of prayer, of liturgical cycles, and of the turning, passing years.

"The nuns who taught in my Catholic grade school handed out holy cards as rewards for everything—from winning the spelling bee to cleaning the blackboards. On very special occasions, such as a birthday or a feast day, we were often given a beautiful gilded image of Mary. Today, I honor these iconic images as I embellish and enrobe Mary in the light of the jewel-like beads, the textures of the rich fabrics, and the shimmer of silk threads.

"Reclaiming these Christian images of the Universal Mother in a powerful, assertive, and feminist way is central to my work. The idea of art—all the arts— as prayer, rather than rote prayer as supplication, is central to reclaiming the power of the feminine in our world. My use of art as prayer embraces Mary in all her manifestations and offers homage and praise to the sacred feminine within us all. I offer these prayers for a restoration of balance and healing in myself, in the world, and in the Roman Catholic Church itself."

MATERIALS

Size 10° silver-lined gold seed beads

Size 11° iridescent gold seed beads

Size 11° translucent seed beads in mix of red, orange, yellow, blue, green, and aqua

Size 11° opaque black hex-cut beads

Size 15° metallic gold seed beads

2½ x 4½" (6.5 x 11 cm) laminated holy card

7½ x 10½" (19 x 26.5 cm) Arches cold-press watercolor paper, 300 lb

16 x 19" (40.5 x 48.5 cm) piece velvet fabric

15¾" (40 cm) velvet binding, 23.5 yd (21.5 m)

16 x 19" (40.5 x 48.5 cm) heavy-weight shirt flannel pieces, 2

Gold Belding Corticelli size A silk thread or other beading thread

Dark gray Belding Corticelli size A silk thread or other beading thread

Sewing thread

Monofilament

⅜" (1 cm) round eye screws, 2

15.5' (4.72 m) ½" wooden dowel

Watercolor paints

Gold metallic acrylic paint

TOOLS

Size 12 beading or sharp needle

Sewing needle

Scissors

Awl and mallet

Self-healing cutting mat

Pencil

Ruler

White, acid-free glue

Chalk

Plate or palette

Paintbrushes

Water container

Cloth

Large brass safety pins

TECHNIQUES

Backstitch (page 155)

Spot stitch (page 155)

PREPARING THE PAPER

Set the card on the mat and punch holes around the card's perimeter with the awl and mallet. The holes should be about ⅛" (3 mm) apart and ¼" (6 mm) in from the plastic edge.

Figure 1

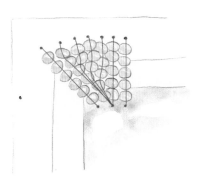

Figure 2

Center the card on the watercolor paper and trace around it. Carefully press the tip of the awl through each of the holes in the card to make small indentations in the paper. Remove the card and punch through each indentation.

Draw straight lines to form wide rays from the center of each side of the tracing. Fill the areas between the rays with straight lines, circles, and wavy lines, playing off the shapes of the image on the card (Figure 1).

Paint the wide-ray segments with gold acrylic. Paint the drawn areas with a variety of complementary colors. Let dry.

Glue the card to the center of the paper, being careful to line up the holes.

Make another series of holes ⅜" (1 cm) from the edge, aligning them with the existing holes to form a second rectangular border around the card. These holes, which will allow you to bead through the paper, should be about ¼" (6 mm) apart. Do not punch holes within the gold rays. Randomly punch holes in the watercolored sections, along the curves and lines between the drawn designs.

In the gold sections of the paper, punch holes ¼" (6 mm) apart along the lines of

the rays. I drew a few more straight lines within the top and bottom rays, then punched holes along and between them, close to the edge of the paper. I also drew large starbursts in the rays on either side of the card.

BEADING THE PAPER

Begin beading with gold 10's and gold thread to frame the card. To make the stitches, pass up through a hole (from back to front) just outside the card. String 5 or 6 beads and pass down through the corresponding hole in the card (Figure 2). Repeat all around the edge of the card, adjusting as needed at the corners to get complete coverage. Backstitch a single line of beads to define the inner and outer edges of this frame.

Next, bead the watercolor portion of the paper. Pass up through the paper (from back to front), string 1 seed bead in the desired color (using the seed-bead color mix and the 15° gold beads), and pass down through the paper (spot stitch). After beading a section, pass through all the beads again to secure. (After the watercolor paper is sewn to the fabric, it's nearly impossible to go back and replace a lost bead or tighten a loose one.)

To bead the gold rays, work backstitch along the straight lines with groups of 3 gold size 11's. When you finish a line, bring the thread up through the hole at one end of the line, pass the thread continuously through the entire line of beads in one pass, and then down the hole at the other end of the line (Figure 3). This stitching is very important because it secures the individual beads and keeps the lines of beads from shifting. Set the beadwork aside.

PREPARING THE BASE

Assemble and handstitch the velvet backing, the double layer of flannel batting, and the velvet front (right sides together). Place large safety pins in the center to stabilize the layers. Fold over the velvet binding to cover all the edges and hemstitch the binding on front and back.

BEADING THE FABRIC

Center the beaded paper on the fabric and mark each corner with chalk.

Carefully hemstitch the watercolor paper through all the layers of fabric. Stitch a densely beaded frame around the paper with the seed-bead mix just as you did to frame the card.

Continue beading outward onto the fabric for 1 to 1½" (2.5 to 3.8 cm). Make 5-bead loops to maintain the same height and density of the beads in the frame. Again, use the seed-bead mix, letting gold beads dominate in the areas beyond the gold rays. The stitching will quilt the fabric. To conceal the thread as you reposition the needle to form loops, pass between the layers of fabric.

Next, change to loops of 3 beads and begin to space the loops randomly ⅛" (3 mm) apart. Continue to let the gold beads dominate on the rays at the top/bottom and right/left of the card.

As you approach the edge of the fabric, change to single, predominantly gold beads. The entire binding is quilted with single beads stitched in place. Stitch a single line of gold beads to bisect each corner of the binding.

Sew the folded strip of cotton binding to the back of the piece along the top edge. Insert the dowel and handstitch the opening closed. Insert an eye screw in each end of the dowel and tie a length of monofilament through the eyes to hang the finished piece.

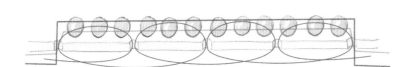

Figure 3

HANDHELD PRAYER BEADS

Eleanor Wiley

"My search for personal truth about God started after the death of my daughter more than thirty years ago. When I was asked to teach a meditation class in 1996, I had already been making necklaces for about two years and knew that stringing beads had a meditative quality. When I looked up the origin of the word 'bead' and found it derived from *biddan*, 'to pray,' it all fell into place. The words of His Holiness, the Dalai Lama, came back to me: 'Look first to your own roots.'

"I believe that the Universe led me to create contemporary prayer beads to be used by all people seeking the Divine. The beads have taught me there is no right way to make personal prayer pieces, and now I have the opportunity to exhibit and teach all over the world. I have been to the Balkans doing peace work, in prisons and hospitals throughout this country, and at interfaith gatherings in India, South Africa, and elsewhere, teaching others to trust their inner truth and create bead pieces that support personal prayer practice. Beads continue to teach me about my life on a daily basis. All I have to do is listen.

"Handheld prayer beads are designed to be kept in a pocket or on a coffee table, nightstand, or desk—as everyday reminders of the spiritual gifts of the ancients who have been with us through the centuries. I created the smaller handheld piece to honor the old world and the new. The scarab is a symbol of Khepera, the Egyptian god of creation, and in Africa it represents the lunar symbol of eternal renewal. The amulet I chose is made of hematite, a stone believed to enhance original thinking. I combined this contemporary scarab with a polymer clay bead to show the beauty of modern materials. I also selected two ancient Greek beads—each an individual sculpture made with primitive tools, a reminder of simplicity. Holding this piece, I am reminded that all materials can be beautiful, whether complex or simple, ancient or contemporary. Creation arises from the spirit.

"The larger handheld piece includes a sterling silver Sacred Wheel of Peace; a pre-Columbian stone bead; a long Angami bead made from the columella of a chank shell from Nagaland, India; an old jasper bead (possibly made in Afghanistan); and a silk tassel.

"The Naga shell bead represents the spiritual myths of the hill tribes of northeast India and Myanmar (Burma). The Sacred Wheel of Peace is a mandala of archetypal symbols that I chose to represent all spiritual paths. When I use this mandala for prayer, I embrace the joys and sorrows of all people. The symbols on the outer edge of the wheel represent rituals and differences. The spokes represent convergence as we learn about each other and ourselves. We all share the quiet space of the hub and can be with each other in silence. The outside edge is inscribed with the phrase 'A place to begin.' We each decide where that place is. The inscription also reminds us that each moment is a place to begin. I combined the wheel with ancient beads traditionally used for prayer to remind us that our ancestors have honored the divine with beads and amulets throughout the ages."

MATERIALS

20" (51 cm) of 1 mm cotton string

1" (2.5cm) hematite scarab bead (or similar)

1" (2.5cm) polymer clay bead (or similar)

Two 15mm rondelle ancient Greek beads (or similar)

10" (25.5 cm) length of 18-gauge silver wire (optional)

Quick-drying glue

TOOLS

Wire cutters

Scissors

TECHNIQUES

Stringing (page 156)

Knots (page 151)

Wirework (page 153)

MAKING THE SMALL STRAND

There are no specific directions for making this small, simple piece. You just have to play. I threaded string through the scarab, making the strands slightly uneven. Then I tied a knot, threaded both strands through the polymer clay bead, and tied another knot below it to hold the bead in place.

I strung the Greek beads on each strand and tied knots big enough to hold them in position. I always put a drop of glue on my knots to secure them. To add a decorative touch to the piece, I wrapped three of the knots with silver wire.

MATERIALS

30" (76 cm) of black 1 mm cotton cord or string

Sacred Wheel of Peace or other amulet

4 or 5 beads of different shapes and sizes

Silk thread (size E or F) or ribbon, in color of choice, for tassel

Quick-drying glue

Tape

TOOLS

Scissors

Small piece of lightweight cardboard

TECHNIQUES

Stringing (page 156)

Knots (page 151)

MAKING THE LARGE STRAND

The most important consideration for this piece is to make sure that the bead you choose to place at the bottom (above the tassel) has a hole big enough for four strands of your cord.

I started by folding the cord in half (you can vary the length to suit your project). Next, I threaded the cord through the center of the wheel (which allows the wheel to spin) and tied a knot.

I strung the first bead and made a knot big enough to hold the bead in place. I continued to add beads, placing a knot between each. Use your own judgment and eye to determine the spacing. When you finish beading, you will have an excess length of cord, which you will use to attach the tassel.

I made my tassel with size F silk thread and worked with a $5 \times 3"$ (12.5×7.5 cm) piece of cardboard. I wrapped three 6"(15 cm) strands around the top of the cardboard. Then I taped the silk thread to the bottom of the board. I wrapped the silk thread on the spool around the cardboard—about 150 to 200 times—to make as large a mound of loops as I wanted for the tassel. Then I tightly tied the loops with the three strands I had wrapped around the top of the card and made several knots. I gently slid the loops off the card and tied a 30" (76 cm) length of silk about ¼" (6 mm) below the top of the bundle. I tightly wrapped the bundle with the rest of the silk strand.

When I was satisfied with the look of the tassel, I tied off the end and put a drop of glue on the knot. When the glue dried, I trimmed the excess silk.

Next, I strung the two strands of black cotton cord protruding from the last bead through the loop at the top of the tassel and then back through the bead. I secured the cotton thread with a half hitch knot and added a drop of glue. When the glue was dry, I trimmed the cord.

BEADED MANDALA

Mary Tafoya

"Psychoanalyst Carl Jung is often credited with bringing the word mandala into the English language. He discovered these sacred circles in the same place I did—Tibetan Buddhist art. I clearly remember the first time I flipped through a book of sacred Tibetan mandalas and painted *thangkas* (sacred scrolls). I fell into a vast and captivating world that was completely foreign to me, whose language and symbolism I didn't understand, but felt compelled to decipher.

"I spent several years studying Tibetan Buddhist art in books and museum collections, researching the names and attributes of deities and sacred symbols, and even learning a bit about how the paints and other materials were made. Though I'm hardly an expert, these images and ideas have been a touchstone for me as I explore and cultivate my artistic expression.

"I was raised Roman Catholic and still practice that tradition. Many years ago, I moved to the Southwest, where Our Lady of Guadalupe has since been a constant and familiar presence in my life. Here in New Mexico, there are many adobe churches and backyard shrines devoted to the Blessed Mother. I also have strong ties to a spiritual community in Mexico City, Mexico. Although the group is not Catholic, it expresses a strong devotion to Our Lady of Guadalupe and makes a pilgrimage to her shrine there each year on December 12, her feast day.

"About twenty years ago, I learned a meditation from a friend, which has served me well in times of trouble and change. Since then, the ending of a relationship, the death of a loved one, marriage difficulties, and the healing of childhood trauma have all been easier to bear with the help of prayer and creative visualization. In developing this mandala, I wanted to combine the important symbolic and spiritual influences in my life into a meditative beadwork project. So I set out to translate these healing ideas into the active ritual of beadwork, creating a piece that is faithful to the style and natural color palette of traditional Tibetan mandalas but that also allows an intimate space for other personal symbols. This mandala helps me concentrate my energies and align all aspects of the self as I move forward through change and turmoil."

MATERIALS

Sizes 6°, 8°–14° assorted seed beads

Accent beads (sequins, Czech fire-polished and pressed-glass beads, crystals, stones)

Small meaningful charms and found objects

Vintage sew-ons, nail heads, metal findings, or other accents

2 sheets 6 × 6" (15 × 15 cm) of thick, nonwoven polyester substrate (I used Bead Backing by Sova Enterprises)

Silamide or other durable beading thread

8 × 8" (20.5 × 20.5 cm) fabric swatch

Clear-drying craft or fabric glue (optional)

Fabric tape, acid-free tape, or tacky glue

8 × 10" (20.5 × 25.5 cm) picture frame, without glass (optional)

8 × 10" (20.5 × 25.5 cm) piece of colored mat board (optional)

TOOLS

Sewing scissors

Pencil, permanent marker, or fabric marker

Beading needles in the appropriate sizes for your beads

Small heat laminator (optional)

Awl or sharp clay needle tool

TECHNIQUES

Bead embroidery (page 155)

Fringes (page 154)

BEFORE YOU BEGIN

Find a quiet, comfortable place and time to work. To help you work intuitively and spontaneously, arrange all your materials so they're within arm's reach—and arrange them in the same way each time you sit down to work. The less time you spend locating your materials, the more time you'll have to be creative.

Choose a palette of several seed bead colors and sizes. Select beads, accents, and colors that evoke the feeling you want to create in the finished piece. Choose more colors than you think you'll need and work with colors that are most meaningful to you. Make a list of personal color symbolisms, relying on your own experiences and preferences.

CUTTING THE BACKING

Photocopy the template on page 94, enlarging it 30 percent (Figure 1). Cut out the 5" (12.5 cm) paper square and trace around it onto the substrate. Cut out the substrate square and set aside. Next, cut out the 4" (10 cm) paper circle, trace it onto the substrate, and cut out the traced circle. You will have two pieces of substrate backing. Cut out the

template triangle and trace its shape inside the substrate circle.

SELECTING SYMBOLS

Select a personal symbol for each point of the triangle. Take a little time to visualize each topic. Remember, this is your mandala, and only your rules apply—you don't have to explain or justify your choices. For the bottom left angle, choose a symbol or image that represents how you see yourself. For the right angle, choose a symbol that represents how you think others see you. For the apex, choose a symbol that represents your concept of the divine.

Now select an accent bead, gemstone, or small treasure to illustrate each symbol. You could also laminate and bead a meaningful image or photograph. To do so, cut out the image or photograph, leaving a little more image area than you think you'll need. Laminate the image (or have it done) and trim away the excess plastic, leaving a border of at least $\frac{1}{16}$" (2 mm). Be careful not to trim away all the sealed plastic. Tack the image to the substrate with a few small stitches, then cover the plastic edges as you bead.

MEDITATIVE BEADING

Before I begin beading, I sometimes light a candle to help me concentrate. (While working on this piece, I burned clove-scented votives of a muted red color that reminded me of the natural pigment colors of Tibetan paint.) Thread a needle with a 3' (91.5 cm) length of thread and knot the end. Leave a 4 to 6" (10 to 15 cm) tail. Beginning at the lower left point of the triangle, attach the symbol you've

chosen to represent how you see yourself. If the object or shape does not have holes, anchor it with a bit of craft glue and secure it with couching stitches. String enough seed beads to cross over the object and into the fabric. Reinforce the beaded thread several times, or branch out to create another anchor thread.

In the lower-right point of the triangle, attach the symbol representing how others see you. Attach the symbol for divinity at the apex. Join the three symbols together with a straight line of beads, following the traced lines of the triangle. Embellish the areas around the symbols. The next phase of the meditation is filling the triangle with beads that represent your concept of light, clarity, and healing. Begin at the bottom and stitch horizontal lines. Mixing bead colors and sizes, I beaded short lines back and forth until I reached the top.

Now that your symbols are united and your triangle is filled with light, you're ready to embellish the rest of the circle. Fill the circle with anything you feel complements the inner triangle—a field of flowers, solid color, rays of light, or shimmering sequins. When I started this piece, I honestly didn't know what to put in this area, but ideas came to me as I worked. Trust your creative process and allow your unconscious to fill in the gaps in your composition.

When you have finished beading the circle, consider adding an edging. An edging provides a finishing touch for the artwork and also creates a boundary, a sense of containment, and a safe space for you while you are doing your inner work. I

5" × 5" square

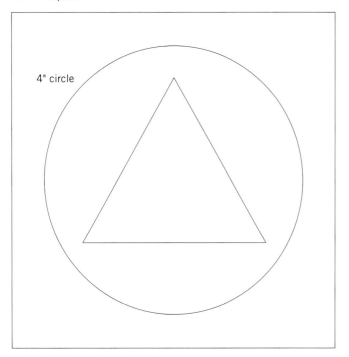

4" circle

Figure 1   Enlarge 30 percent

Figure 2

Figure 3

selected a pointed edging that suggests rays of light (Figure 2).

BACKING THE CIRCLE

Lay the fabric swatch over the substrate and wrap it around to the back. Secure it with a bit of fabric tape—or if the fabric is heavy enough so the stitches won't show on the front of the work, sew it to the substrate.

Center the circle on the fabric-covered square. Make small tacking stitches every inch or so near the edge of the circle.

ADDING FRINGE

If you decide to add fringe, select about 24 accent beads or precious objects to create the dangles. (You may not use them all, but it's better to have too many on hand than too few.)

Cut a long length of thread and knot the end. Pass from back to front at the center bottom of the square. Make a simple fringe leg. Then sew through the fabric from front to back, in the same spot you began. (If you're planning to mount the mandala in a frame, the fringe should be no more than about 2" [5 cm] long.)

Continue adding fringe legs until you reach the edge of the fabric square. Tie a secure knot at the back of the square and trim the thread. Cut a new length of thread and add fringe to the other half of the square in the same way.

MOUNTING THE MANDALA

To hang the mandala, you can simply stitch the fabric-covered square to a rectangle of fabric that has been hemmed at top and bottom. Then slip wooden dowels inside the hems to support and weight the top and bottom edges of the piece (Figure 3).

You can also frame the mandala. To do so, remove the glass from the frame. Trace

the outline of the fabric-covered square onto the back of the mat board. If you've worked with my template, position the square $1\frac{1}{2}$" (3.8 cm) from the top, $1\frac{1}{2}$" (3.8 cm) from the left and right sides, and $3\frac{1}{2}$" (9 cm) from the bottom of the board.

Punch a small hole through the mat board in each corner of the traced square with the awl or needle tool. If your mandala is larger than the template, punch extra holes along the sides.

Tie a size 6° or 8° stopper bead to the end of a length of thread with a single overhand knot. Place the fabric-covered square on top of the mat board. Bring the threaded needle up through one of the corner holes in the mat board and through the square. If you'd like, attach a sequin, seed bead, or accent bead. Take a small stitch through the fabric and back down through the hole in the mat board. Tie the thread ends around the stopper bead with a square knot and trim (Figure 4). Stitch beads through the remaining holes in the same way, using a separate thread for each.

Figure 4

THREE BEADED PRAYERS

Sonya Clark
Stephenie Goodwin

"I created the concept of *The Beaded Prayers Project* [page 146] as a way to bring people together at the most human level. I first found amulets filled with prayer and powerful medicines while I was traveling in West Africa ten years earlier. The African amulets provided the initial inspiration for the project. But as I researched widely and talked to those with other ethnic backgrounds, I found similar amulets in traditions throughout the world.

"These two beaded prayers contain secret messages, but their exteriors reveal my interest in chromatic symbolism. Among the Yoruba in Nigeria, the color red signifies *ashe*, the power to make things happen. Like the blood that courses through our bodies, ashe is the connection between all living things. It is life force. Black and gold complement the red. The black signifies mystery and the unknown. The yellow and gold signify the wealth that comes with wisdom or revelation. I worked with silk cloth because silk is associated with transformation, as in the transformation of a silkworm to a moth. The glass and brass beads celebrate the shared etymology of the words 'bead' and 'prayer.'"

—*Sonya Clark*

"'Many candles can be kindled from one candle without diminishing it' are the words written inside my beaded prayer. The phrase comes from the Talmud, a collection of writings that help the Jewish people understand their legal and moral responsibilities according to the Torah, the Jewish holy scriptures. I chose this phrase as my written blessing for its symbolic reference to the continuous inspiration and kindling of faith from one generation to the next among Jewish people.

"I enclosed the blessing in leather, the same material used in the historic amulets, or *kemi'ot*, of the Jewish people to protect a written prayer. I also added fringe to the double-beaded edge stitching. The fringe refers to the *tallit*, a Jewish prayer shawl with blue stripes and fringe. The long knotted fringe, called *tzitzit*, hangs at the four corners of the shawl, as directed by the Torah. The color blue, seen in various shades in the beaded fringe, is a representation of an ancient dye mentioned in the Torah that was used to dye a thread in the *tzitzit*."

—Stephenie Goodwin

MATERIALS

For each of the three beaded prayers

5 × 5" (12.5 × 12.5 cm) piece of silk, other woven cloth, or leather (for rectangular prayer only)

5" (12.5 cm) ribbon, 2 lengths (for taffy-style beaded prayer only)

Size 6° beads, 12" (30.5 cm) strand

Size 11° beads, 12" (30.5 cm) strand

Size B or D Nymo beading thread

Additional beads for fringe (optional)

8½ × 11" (21.5 × 28 cm) sheet of paper

TOOLS

Size 10 beading needle

Scissors

TECHNIQUES

Fringes (page 154)

Bead embroidery (page 155)

MAKING THE TAFFY-STYLE BEADED PRAYER

Write your wish, dream, or prayer on the piece of paper. Hold the paper in portrait position and fold it in half horizontally. Fold it in half vertically and then fold it in half vertically again. Roll the paper to make a small bundle (Figure 1). Enclose the paper in the piece of cloth. Twist both ends and tie each with ribbon. Use spot or seed-stitch bead embroidery to embellish the surface with rows of randomly placed beads. Decorate the edges of the beaded prayer with a single beaded edge stitch (Figure 2).

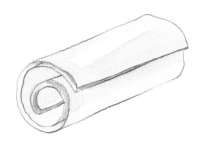

Figure 1

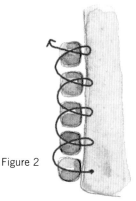

Figure 2

MAKING THE RECTANGULAR BEADED PRAYERS

Write your wish, dream, or prayer on the piece of paper. Fold the prayer as you would for the taffy-style version, but don't roll it. Place the folded paper in the center of the piece of cloth or leather. Fold the long parallel edges of the cloth toward the center (Figure 3).

Then fold the short parallel edges of the cloth toward the center (Figure 4). Fold the entire packet in half widthwise (Figure 5).

Seal and decorate the edges of the packet with double-beaded edge stitch, as follows: Secure the thread to the cloth with several stitches. String 3 beads and stitch through the cloth so that the first and last beads sit on the edge of the cloth, side-to-side, and then stitch back through the third bead. Add 2 more beads. Stitch through the cloth and then back through the second bead. Repeat, adding 2 beads at a time as you stitch around the edge of the packet (Figure 6). Add decorative fringe if desired.

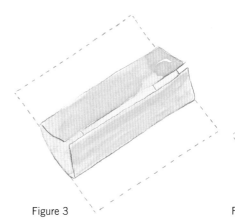

Figure 3

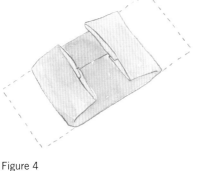

Figure 4

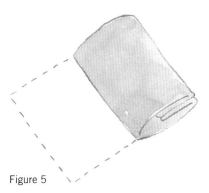

Figure 5

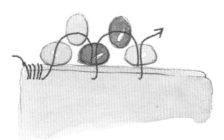

Figure 6

chapter six

BEADING FOR BONDING

Beads speak their own language. As gifts and ritual objects, they can extend warm greetings, express joy, and convey deep affection. Beadwork has long been a way to reach out to others, in both personal and communal gestures. The message may lie within the beads, the colors, or the pattern. But the true message lies in the thought and care of the maker who, bead by bead, gives the object its meaning.

The Zulu women of South Africa bead messages of love in the decorative designs in a style of necklace called an *ibheqe*. These multicolor, tabbed necklaces are also known as love letters. The colors and triangular patterns are a system of encoded language, truly known only to the maker and the recipient. Even the material of the bead—whether glass or plastic—may speak volumes.

Each of the Zulu's traditional seven colors has both a negative and positive connotation—although white, a symbol of purity, is always positive. The Zulu vocabulary of color equates red with passion or anger, green with contentment or discord. But the true meaning comes from the specific combinations of colors, beads, and shapes.

Beads are also significant in the rituals of marriages, among the Zulu and other people. Strands of white beads are worn to signify a Zulu engagement, and gifts of beads welcome the bride into the family of the groom. One of the first gifts a Xhosa man gives the woman he hopes to marry is a strand of beads.

An Ndebele bride wears an elaborate wedding costume—a glass-beaded apron and cape, a back veil that cascades to the ground, and a dense front veil of multiple beaded strands. The Xhosa bride and groom both wear beads. A bridegroom in Gujarat, India, wears a mask of beaded strands, sometimes with shells, suspended from a bead-embroidered band.

Some Indian brides wear a traditional necklace of black beads and gold, a style of *mangalsutra*, Sanskrit for "auspicious thread." The necklace is a gift from the groom's family. The black beads are believed to ward off the Evil Eye. In some regions of India, the beads are coral. During the ceremony, the groom ties the two strands of the necklace—a custom similar to the Japanese Buddhist wedding practice of interweaving two strings of beads to symbolize the joining of families.

The state of Gujarat in western India is known for its folk embroidery, which is often decorated with beadwork, mirrors, sequins, buttons, and shells. A bride has many such textiles in her dowry, including embellishments for the home. In the districts of Saurashtra and Kutch, a *toran*, a rectangular or arch-shaped decorative hanging, is traditionally hung above the main doorway. It serves as a sign of welcome to all visitors who enter the house, whether they are human and divine. Ganesh, the elephant-headed god who removes obstacles to happiness, is often a featured motif. A bride may also make a beaded toran for her wedding bed.

Single and married Zulu women create beaded necklaces for the men in their lives. They arrange the colors and patterns to create a coded message, best understood by the parties involved. A triangle whose apex points down signifies a man; one whose apex points up signifies a woman. Joined triangles represent married men and women. From the collection of Helen Banes.

In the Polynesian islands, necklaces called leis are traditionally worn for wedding celebrations and other important events. Although often made from flowers and feathers, early leis were also made from teeth, bones, seeds, and shells. In early societies, shell bracelets and necklaces were exchanged as currency and as gifts between island tribes. During the nineteenth century, shell leis became popular as personal embellishment and as gifts to welcome friends and honor prominent visitors.

Some of the most prized Hawaiian leis are made with the species of fine-quality shells found in abundance on the island of Niihau. Because of their color and shape, the tiny, pearl-like *laiki* shells from Niihau are also called rice shells. Strands of laiki, joined with a cowrie shell, are the traditional style of lei worn at weddings.

The practice of giving gifts is central to Native American culture. Traditionally, a person's stature was measured by his generosity, and his wealth by what he had to give. In the Northwest Coast culture and others, beaded garments and other valued objects were distributed in ceremonial giveaways called potlatches. Among the gift items were beaded bags filled with food. The gift recipient would later refill the bag and give it away again—to continue the important cycle of mutual support.

Friends within or across native tribes exchanged beaded bracelets as tokens of affection. Families about to be joined by a marriage gave each other gifts of shell beads and beaded bags. Tribal leaders also exchanged beaded objects in gestures of good will and as promises of peaceful coexistence.

The desire to connect with others in meaningful ways is a basic human impulse, essential to our lives and society. Moved by that pleasurable impulse, the designers in this chapter have, through their beadwork, reached out to friends and family members. In the process of making objects for others, they have often found themselves, surprisingly yet inevitably, also on the receiving end.

A Chinese bride wears an elaborate headdress called a phoenix crown—symbol of the empress—decorated with pearls and the bright blue feathers of the kingfisher. The veil of this crown is made of strands of pearls. Pearls are associated with wisdom and with the celestial dragon, a symbol of the emperor. The mythical, colorful phoenix also symbolizes music and virtue. Together, the two creatures ensure a harmonious union. Photo courtesy of the Minneapolis Institute of Arts, the John R. Van Derlip Fund (8" [20.36 cm] depth at crown).

WEDDING SHAWL

Eleanor Wiley

"I made this wedding shawl of prayer beads for a couple who decided to renew their wedding vows after fifteen years of marriage. They included their daughter in the ceremony, so I made a separate beaded strand for each—wife, husband, and daughter. Each person carried a strand, and the three strands were joined together during the ceremony. The beads are now on display in the couple's home as a house blessing.

"In the strands, I included amulets from each family member and special symbols that represent each person. The wife's strand contains moonstone and sterling silver with female amulets, dragonflies, hearts, and charms from her childhood. The husband's strand contains mother-of-pearl, moonstone, sterling silver, fish amulets, and his father's military dog tags. The daughter's strand contains mother-of-pearl, clear glass and sterling beads, fairy amulets, beads that belonged to her great-grandmother, and her father's keepsake baby beads. I chose pearls as the primary beads in all three strands because they are the Greek symbol of love.

"Each strand is connected by a beaded loop to the silver knot I made by hammering and polishing half-hard silver. The joined strands symbolize how we each can retain our individuality but still come together to create a new whole. This wedding shawl, which can be hung on a wall or worn around the neck—open or clasped with a pin—serves to remind the participants of their joining together and of the important vows they have made to each other."

MATERIALS

For a child's 18" strand

Assorted meaningful beads and amulets

30–50 seed beads for each amulet loop

2 jump rings for each amulet (1 unsoldered, 1 soldered)

2 crimp beads for each amulet loop

Heavy-gauge sterling silver wire

32" (81.5 cm) beading wire (6–8" for each amulet)

TOOLS

Needle-nose or crimp pliers

Wire cutters

Heavy-duty pliers

Jeweler's hammer

Polishing cloth

TECHNIQUES

Stringing (page 156)

Crimping (page 156)

Wirework (page 153)

Knots (page 151)

MAKING THE CHILD'S STRAND

There is no right way to make prayer beads. These directions just provide a guide to help get you started. Feel free to invent your own methods along the way. It's wonderful to experiment and try new ideas!

I started by making the child's strand for the shawl. Cut a 24" (61 cm) length of beading wire. String 2 crimp beads and enough seed beads so that the loop will slip over the largest amulet you plan to add at the end of the main strand (Figure 1). Pass back through the crimp beads, snug the beads, and crimp. This is the loop you will attach to the silver knot in the final step.

To make the body of the piece, string beads and amulets for about 14" (35.5 cm)—you can play with this number depending on your design. For the child's strand, I chose antique mother-of-pearl, clear glass, and sterling silver disks. Fairies were the primary amulets, and I added them randomly throughout the pattern. Add the amulets by first attaching an unsoldered jump ring to the amulet. Then string a soldered jump ring on the strand and attach the two jump rings. The small chain made by the jump rings allows each amulet to move freely.

When you are about 5" (12.5 cm) from the end of the wire, string 2 crimp beads. Next, decide how many amulet loops you wish to add at the end of the strand. For each loop, string 2 more crimp beads. Do not crimp.

String enough seed beads and an amulet to make the first loop. Pass back through all the crimp beads, snug all the beads on the main strand, and secure only the first 2 crimp beads.

To create each additional amulet loop, cut a short strand of beading wire and string seed beads and the amulet. Decide how long you would like the loop to be—I make them uneven so they fall at different levels. Pass both wire ends back through a set of 2 crimp beads on the main strand and crimp (Figure 2). As you add the loops, check the strength of each crimp by giving the loop a slight tug. If it moves, the crimp is not tight enough.

MAKING THE ADULT STRANDS

Create the additional strands for the shawl in the same way, working to the length you choose, with whatever beads and amulets you like.

ATTACHING THE STRANDS

Next, bend a length of sterling silver wire with heavy-duty pliers to make a free-form "knot" to attach the other strands. Gently hammer to harden it, then polish. If you want to experiment, start with copper wire (it's cheaper and easier to bend). Just play around and see what happens.

Join the main strand to the wire knot by making a lark's head knot with the initial seed-bead loop.

Figure 1

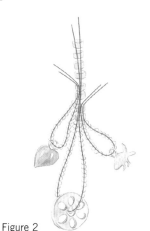

Figure 2

DOUBLE-STRAND BRIDAL NECKLACE

Laura McCabe

"I designed this simple, yet meaningful, pearl necklace for a bride. Pearls have long been associated with the protection of women and are a symbol of all things feminine, beauty, and fertility. I have also made bridal necklaces with symbols of the moon and the ocean, such as shell, mother-of-pearl, and moonstone (a traditional gift for lovers). By changing the colors of the beads and pearls, you can customize the necklace to suit the preferences of the bride who will wear it. I try to bring in a personal aspect of the bride's life, too. For example, my friend Cori loves the ocean and boating, so I designed her bridal necklace around the motif of sea anemones.

"The forget-me-not embroidery on the back of this cabochon is particularly dear and harkens back to the traditions of the Victorian era, when the flower was a symbol of true love. The bead embroidery also provides 'something blue'—a necessity for every bride. I sometimes embroider the initials of the bride and the groom or the date of the wedding on the back of the piece, so the writing is concealed and known only to the wearer, just as it is inside a wedding band.

"I often add a dangling bezeled cabochon at the back of the necklace to provide a decorative detail that is visible when the bride's back is turned. She can later remove the cabochon and wear a less ornate version of her bridal necklace anytime she wants to.

"I've created many bridal necklaces, but because they are so personal, they have all been gifts for people I know—friends and relatives, including my sister, Meg. And making a necklace is also a cool way to be part of the wedding celebration!"

MAKING THE BEZEL

Apply an even coat of adhesive to the back side of the mabe pearl with a toothpick. Glue the pearl to the center of one of the leather pieces. Let dry.

Knot the end of a 5' (152.5 cm) length of waxed thread and pass up through the leather, next to the pearl. String 6 Delicas and line them up flush against the pearl. Pass back down through the leather after the sixth bead and back up between the third and fourth beads; pass through the last 3 beads again. Continue working backstitch around the base of the pearl.

The finished round should have an even number of beads. Weave through the round again to reinforce and line up the beads.

Use Delicas to work two or more rounds of tubular peyote stitch off the backstitched base round. To shape the bezel to fit the pearl, switch to size 15° seed beads so the bezel automatically draws in without a decrease.

When the bezel is as high as you want it to be, weave the thread back down through the rounds of peyote stitch until you reach the first round. Pass

back through the leather and make a knot close to the leather. There's no need to cut the thread—you'll have enough left to complete the next step.

Pass back up through the leather, right next to the beaded bezel. String 6 Delicas and begin a second round of beaded backstitching around the bezel. Be sure this round has an even number of beads. Pass back through the leather, knot to secure, and trim the thread.

FORGET-ME-NOT EMBROIDERY

The bead embroidery on the back of the cabochon is optional, but it provides a

MATERIALS

1" (2.5 cm) mabe pearl

5 g each of 2 colors size 11° Delicas

5 g each of 3–5 colors size 15° Japanese seed beads

5 g each of 2 colors size 11° Japanese seed beads

50 faceted rondelle 4mm glass beads

Two 16" (40.5 cm) strands of pearls, each a different color or size

2 pieces of leather, about 2 x 2" (5 x 5 cm) each

Antique button for closure

Nymo D or other beading thread in a color to match your beads

E-6000 glue

Toothpicks

Microcrystalline wax or beeswax

For the forget-me-not embroidery (optional)

Size 11° Japanese seed beads in gold luster or yellow for embroidery

Size 15° Japanese seed beads in bright blue and green for embroidery

TOOLS

Size 12° English beading needles

Embroidery scissors

TECHNIQUES

Backstitch (page 155)

Tubular peyote stitch (page 153)

Whipstitch (page 155)

Stringing (page 156)

Knots (page 151)

Figure 1

Figure 2

Figure 3

nice detail. Embroider the floral design on the second piece of leather, working with size 15° and 11° seed beads (Figure 1). When you embroider with beads, be sure to pass back through the beads several times after they have been stitched down. The extra reinforcement will hold the beads tightly in place to create a nice, neat look.

BACKING THE MABE PEARL

To back the mabe pearl with the second piece of leather, start a new thread with a knot in the end and pass up through the first piece of leather, between the bezel and the outer round of the backstitch.

Apply an even coat of adhesive to the back of the bezeled pearl, extending the glue beyond the outer round of backstitch. Then place the second piece of leather over the glued area, with the embroidered side out. Press firmly and let dry.

Carefully cut around the cabochon through both layers of leather. Be sure to leave about one bead's width of leather edging to ensure you don't cut through any of your stitching. Stitch through the leather to the back of the cabochon and whipstitch around the

entire perimeter. Exit between the bezel and the outer round of backstitch.

Pass through a couple of beads in the outer round of backstitch. Use Delicas to work one round of peyote stitch and size 11° seed beads to work two additional rounds. Change colors with each round or, if you prefer, keep the color the same.

CREATING THE BAIL

Working with the same thread, weave up to the top edge of the piece. Create a bail by working a tab of flat even-count peyote stitch that extends off the outer round of backstitched Delicas. The tab should be 6 to 8 beads wide and 24 to 28 beads long.

Attach the end of the tab to the first round of peyote stitch you worked off the base. The loop serves as a bail for the pendant.

Embellish the edge of the bail with picots. To do so, exit from a Delica bead, string 3 size 15° seed beads, and then pass back down into the next Delica bead (Figure 2). When you have edged both sides of the bail, secure the thread and trim.

STRINGING THE NECKLACE

The first strand of the necklace is made entirely of pearls and size 11° seed beads. By placing a size 11° bead between pairs of pearls, you can create the look of knotted pearls without having to do all the extra work.

Cut two 3' (91.5 cm) lengths of thread and thread a needle on each. Pair the needles together and, leaving a 6" (15 cm) tail, string 1 size 11°, 1 pearl, 1 size 11°, 1 pearl, 1 size 11°, 1 pearl, 5 size 11°s, 1 pearl, the button, 1 pearl, and 5 size 11°s. Pass back through the last pearl and make a half hitch knot around the main thread. Pass back through the next 2 beads and make another knot. Continue making knots between beads until you get to the first bead you strung (Figure 3).

Separate the two needles. On the first strand, continue stringing for 8½" (21.5 cm) by alternating pearls and size 11°s. For the second strand, work with the pearls that are a different color or size. String 1 pearl, 1 size 15°, 1 rondelle, and 1 size 15°. Repeat until this strand is a little longer than the first one to give the finished necklace a scalloped look.

When the strands are long enough for the first half of the necklace, bring the two needles together and string 10 size 11°s and the pendant. The pendant will slide over the seed beads.

Separate the two needles again and string the second half of the necklace to match the first half. When you reach the portion of the necklace where the two strands turn back into one, bring the needles together and string 1 size 11°, 1 pearl, 1 size 11°, 1 pearl, 1 size 11°, 1 pearl, and enough size 11°s to comfortably fit over the button. Pass back through the last pearl you added and make a half hitch knot around the main thread. Continue down the strand, knotting between beads as you did before. Trim all thread tails close to the beads.

FRENCH BEADED ROSES

Donna DeAngelis Dickt

"For all of us, the holidays are full of traditions and customs that are unique and meaningful. In our family, the Thanksgiving holiday and the advent of the Christmas season were marked for many years by the tradition of the annual, local performance of *The Nutcracker*. For me, there was always something magical about the ballet, no matter how big or small the production. Nothing, however, could be more magical than seeing your own child perform in *The Nutcracker* for the first time on a big stage.

"I'm not quite sure where the tradition of giving roses to a dancer after a performance began—but it's very nice. Before the performance, the director of my daughter's dance company gave each dancer a rose as a token of appreciation. And of course, every parent of every child on that stage sat in the audience waiting with beautiful bouquets of roses to be delivered afterward to mark the special occasion.

"I was no exception. But my daughter's roses were not traditional roses. They were made of beads. My daughter's passion for dancing coincided with a newfound passion of my own—French beaded flowers. I had actually first learned to make beaded flowers from my grandmother about thirty years earlier, but I had then learned only the basics, enough to make a few small flowers. After all those years, I tried beading again and produced a silver wreath scattered with white pearls. (I still hang that wreath every Christmas.) My second attempt was the small bouquet of pink roses I gave to my daughter after her performance. I made it with vintage pink beads that belonged to my grandmother, and I worked from a pattern in an old book she had used. Luckily, little girls think that beads are spectacular, and my daughter was thrilled with her nontraditional bouquet.

"These tea roses were inspired by the roses I made for my daughter's *Nutcracker* performance years ago. Since then, I have taught her how to make beaded flowers for herself. Whenever she needs a special gift for a good friend, she beads a rose. Here we are, thirty-five years after my grandmother helped me to shape my first petal, carrying on a very special tradition of our own."

MATERIALS

For one tea rose

Size 11° or size 9° three-cut seed beads, 1 hank of petal color

Size 11° or size 9° three-cut seed beads, 1 hank of green

20-yd (18.288 m) spool of 24- or 26-gauge colored copper wire in petal color and in green

1 piece of 18-gauge green stem wire, for assembly

1 spool of 30-gauge green or silver paddle wire or 28-gauge craft wire

Green floral tape

TOOLS

Ruler

Wire cutters

Round-nose pliers

Bead Spinner (optional)

TECHNIQUES

French wire beading

MAKING THE ROSE PETALS

Pattern

Make 2 Basic 6, 9 rows, round bottom, round top

Trim petal stems so one long wire extends.

Make 5 Basic 6, 11 rows, round bottom, round top

Trim petal stems so one long wire extends.

String 15" (38 cm) of petal-colored beads onto the petal-colored wire, either directly from the hanks or with a Bead Spinner. Do not cut the wire from the spool. Knot the end of the wire so the beads don't slip off. Slide 6 beads toward the knot. Hold your thumb and forefinger 3" (7.5 cm) from the end of the knot to prevent the beads from slipping. Cross the bare spool wire to make a loop large enough to fit four fingers through. Secure the loop by twisting the wire tightly together ten times.

Hold the wire so the loop is at the bottom and the section with the beads (the basic wire) and the short twisted section (the stem) are in a straight line (Figure 1).

Bend the spool wire up against the 6 beads on the basic wire. Slide down

enough beads to make a second row. Hold both rows of beads firmly near the top and cross the bare spool wire in front of the basic wire at a 90° angle (Figure 2). Bring the bare wire around to the back, then cross in front again to make a complete wrap, always maintaining the 90° angle.

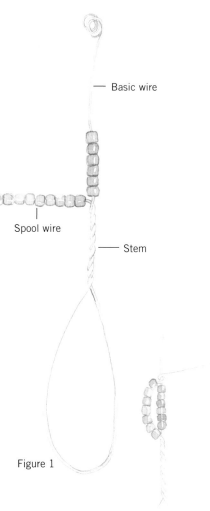

Basic wire

Spool wire

Stem

Figure 1

Figure 2

Figure 3

Figure 4

Turn the petal upside down so the stem wire is now at the top and the basic wire is at the bottom. Slide more beads up to the basic wire and make a wrap (Figure 3).

Continue working the petal this way until you have completed 9 rows. Always keep the petal's face toward you when you turn it upside down so the wire wraps are on the "wrong" side. After completing the last row, twist the spool wire around the stem wire three times to meet the top of the loop. Hold the bare spool wire and cut it 1 to 1½" (2.5 to 3.8 cm) from the petal (Figure 4). Immediately make a knot at the end of the spool wire so you don't spill any beads.

Cut one side of the loop wire about 2" (5 cm) from the petal. You will now have three separate lengths of wire. Straighten the longer loop wire and twist all three wires together to form a tapered stem.

Cut the basic wire at the top of the petal ⅛" (3 mm) from the tip of the petal. Use the pliers to bend the wire flat against the wrong side of the petal.

Make all seven petals for each rose in the same way. The first two petals each

have 9 rows of beads, the others each have 11.

MAKING THE LEAVES

Pattern

Make 1 Basic 3, 11 rows, round bottom, pointed top

Trim leaf stem so one long wire extends.

Make 2 Basic 3, 9 rows, round bottom, pointed top

Trim leaf stem so one long wire extends.

Working with the spool of green wire, string 11" (28 cm) of green beads, but do not cut the wire from the spool. Make the basic wire as before, this time with 3 beads as the basic. Slide up enough beads to make a second row that will fit closely next to the 3 basic beads, but do not wrap the wire yet—this time you will make a pointed tip. Wrap the spool wire across the basic wire at a 45° angle, around the back, to the front, over, and down at another 45° angle. Make the wrap slightly above the last bead at the top of the second row.

To make the next row, slide more beads up to the stem wire. Make sure 1 bead sits at the point of the leaf, in the space you left when you wrapped the wire (Figure 5).

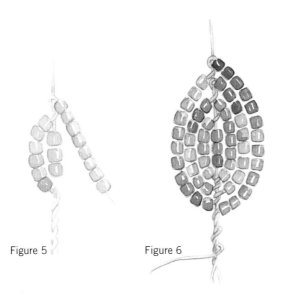

Figure 5

Figure 6

Turn the leaf so the loop end is at the top. On this end of the leaf (the bottom), make a 90° angle wrap, as for the rose petals.

Continue adding rows of beads, creating a point at the top of the leaf and rounding the bottom (Figure 6), until you've added 9 rows of beads. Finish the leaf as you did the petals.

Make all three leaves the same way. Two leaves will have 9 rows, one will have 11.

SEPALS

You will need 3" (7.5 cm) of green beads on the green spool wire for each of the five sepals.

Make the sepal in the same way you made the leaf, but this time the basic is made up of 1" (2.5 cm) of beads. Each sepal is only 3 rows wide (Figure 7).

Gently twist the top half of the sepal twice, allowing the bottom half to remain

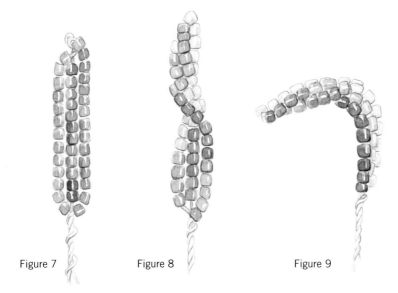

Figure 7

Figure 8

Figure 9

Pattern

Make 5 Basic 1 inch, 3 rows, round bottom, pointed top

Trim sepals so one long wire extends.

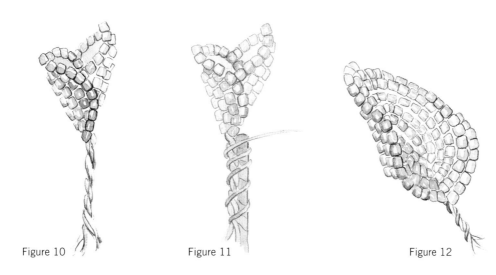

Figure 10   Figure 11   Figure 12

flat (Figure 8). Now gently curve the sepal so that the front of the sepal is on the top of the curve (Figure 9).

ASSEMBLY

Cut the stem wire to the desired finished flower length. Starting at about $\frac{1}{2}$ to 1" (1.3 to 2.5 cm) from the top, wrap to the top of the stem wire with the floral tape. Pull the tape at an angle so it sticks securely. When you get to the top, turn around and wrap to the other end. This is your main stem.

Fold each of the smallest petals in half, with the right sides facing out. Interlock the edges of the petals, with

wrong sides facing each other. Twist the two individual stem wires together to form one stem (Figure 10). Place the twisted petal stem against the main stem so the two petals are positioned just above the end of the main stem. Starting about 1" (2.5 cm) below the petal stem, use the 30-gauge paddle wire or 28-gauge craft wire to wrap the petal and main stems together. End the wrap just beneath the petals (Figure 11). Do not cut the assembly wire from the spool.

Before adding the remaining petals, curve each as shown so that the right side of the petal (the side that does not

show the wire wraps around the basic wire) is on the inside of the curve (Figure 12).

Continue adding petals one at a time, with the right sides facing toward the center of the flower. Attach the petals by securely wrapping the stems with the paddle wire. Overlap each petal slightly to form a circle around the interlocked center petals.

When you've attached the last petal, wrap paddle wire from the base of the flower about $\frac{1}{4}$" (6 mm) down the main stem and cut the wire from the spool. Trim the petal-stem wires to

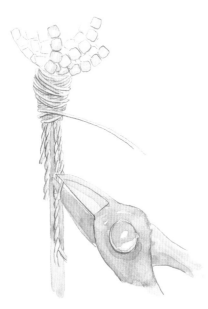

Figure 13

Figure 14

Make a branch of leaves. Begin by taping the stem of the largest leaf with floral tape from the base of the leaf to the end. Bend one of the small leaves so it is at a right angle to the stem and wrap with tape to attach it about $\frac{1}{2}$" (1.3 cm) below the large leaf (Figure 14). Attach the remaining leaf at a right angle to the stem, opposite the other small leaf. Wrap the tape down the length of the stem. Now attach the branch of leaves to the main flower stem, leaving a 1 to $1\frac{1}{2}$" (2.5 to 3.8 cm) stem at the bottom of the branch. Curve the leaves, sepals, and petals to give the flower a natural appearance.

reduce the bulk around the main stem. Stagger the length of the wires so there won't be a ridge when you tape the main stem (Figure 13). Wrap tape from the base of the flower to the middle of the main stem.

Position one sepal under each petal. The right side of the sepal should be facing the petals. Attach the sepals one at a time with floral tape, circling the main stem once as you add each one. When

you've attached all five sepals to the flower, trim the sepal stem wires to reduce bulk on the main stem. Continue taping down the remaining length of the sepal stems to cover the wires. Shape the sepals by bending each one to curve away from the flower.

HEIRLOOM CUBE

Julia Pretl

"*Heirloom* is about the weaving together of family and time. It is about holding tight to past generations while anticipating future ones.

"I began this piece by attaching an old photograph of my grandmother to the fabric. As I sewed the beads on one by one, I found myself reflecting upon what she meant to me. My 'Nanny' died last summer, and I miss her dearly. She was the funniest and most wonderful person I've ever known. Strangely, I do not see my grandmother in this picture. She was very young when it was taken (probably in her early twenties), and I found it both fascinating and sad that she had a whole other life before I, or even my mother, entered her life.

"Next I beaded the panel showing a photograph of my mother. My mom is my best friend, and from the time I was very small I have been aware that our relationship is a special one. We are still able to talk for hours on end, laughing more than anything else. I find it interesting that as I have grown and matured, the difference in my mother's age and mine seems to grow smaller. She now comes to me for advice and to be consoled as often as I go to her. Although I resemble my mother very little in appearance, she passed on to me her strange sense of humor, her love for art, and her deep-set eyes.

"It felt a little strange affixing my own image to the fabric. I'm not used to intentionally memorializing myself. As I worked I realized that, at the time this picture was taken, I was ten to fifteen years older than were my mother or grandmother in their photographs. To my eye, I look younger, and I still can't figure out the reason why.

"I finished my box with a picture of my firstborn daughter, Olive. I often found myself forgetting to bead, instead staring at her picture and marveling at what a lovely young woman she has become, shaking my head at the realization that she is no longer a child. So far, she is showing a great love of art—something that makes me indescribably happy. She has enjoyed watching the progress of this creation and delights in the knowledge that it will belong to her once she is grown.

MATERIALS

Piece of Ultrasuede or other fabric (large enough for four adjacent box sides and for top and lid lining)

Sheet of plastic needlework canvas (large enough to provide for five squares, including the bottom, or six squares if you want to make a lid)

1 or more small photographs

2-oz package of polymer clay

Size 8° seed beads in assorted colors

Size 11° seed beads in assorted colors

Size 15° seed beads in assorted colors

Beading thread

Acid-free glue

TOOLS

Beading needles

Scissors

Ruler

Pencil

X-acto knife

Needle and thread

TECHNIQUES

Backstitch (page 155)

"I created a woven 'roof' for the lid, which was somehow comforting to me and made my treasure feel complete. I asked my mother to find some small item, given to her by her mother, that has importance in her life, to put inside the box. I will do the same, as will my daughter. My hope is that, while reflecting on this box and the treasures it holds, she will remember how those who came before her shaped her life and made her what she has become and how they will influence her in what she is still becoming."

PREPARING THE CANVAS

Decide how large you want each of the four sides of the box to be (mine are 4" [10 cm]). With a ruler and pencil, measure and draw four adjoining squares on the fabric. Cut out the shape, leaving a ¼" (6 mm) border (Figure 1). Do not cut apart the squares.

PREPARING THE PHOTOGRAPH CABOCHONS

Roll out a thin sheet of polymer clay (about ⅛" [3 mm] thick) and cut the desired shape(s) for the photograph(s). Bake the shapes according to the directions on the polymer clay package. When the shapes are cool, trace them onto the photographs. Cut out the photo shapes and glue them to the clay. When the glue has set, center and glue the first photo cabochon on one of the squares you've drawn on the fabric.

MAKING A BEZEL

Thread a needle and tie a knot close to the end of the thread. Sew through the fabric from back to front so it exits about 1/16" (2 mm) from the edge of the cabochon. Pick up 1 size 8° and 1 size 11°. Pass back through the size 8° and through the fabric. The beads should form a picot along the edge of the cabochon. Continue adding picots around the cabochon, making sure the sides of

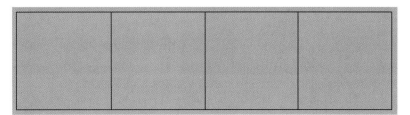

Figure 1

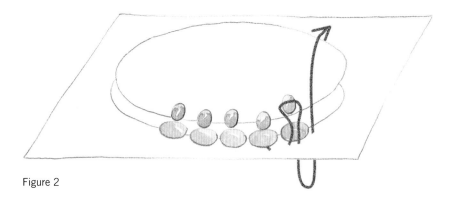

Figure 2

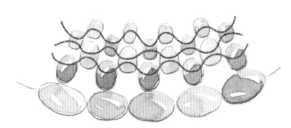

Figure 3

the size 8°s touch each other (Figure 2). To finish the round, pass up through the first two beads added in the round.

Using peyote stitch and tight tension, bead a second round with size 11°s. The beads will begin to pull over the cabochon. Bead a third peyote-stitched round using size 15°s. If necessary for the size of your cabochon, work a fourth round (Figure 3). When the cabochon is secure, weave back through the rounds and into the fabric. Secure the thread. Repeat this process to create bezels for the remaining cabochons.

DECORATING THE FABRIC

Embellish the remaining fabric as much or as little as you'd like with backstitch bead embroidery. Begin by drawing a design on the front of the fabric. Keep in mind that it will be easier to bend the beadwork into a box shape if you bead each square individually.

Fold under the fabric border and stitch it down to finish the edges. Sew the short ends together to create a continuous loop.

BUILDING THE BOX SUPPORT

Now cut five squares from the needle-point canvas. These will make up the four sides and the bottom of the box (Figure 4). Cut a sixth square if you want to make a lid. You may have to experiment a bit, keeping in mind that the sides of the needlepoint box will need to be slightly smaller than the fabric loop. Sew the canvas squares together at the edges to form the box. Slide the embellished fabric over the box and adjust the position so that the corners of the beadwork and box align. Whipstitch the top edge, joining the beaded fabric to the canvas.

I made a lid for my box and glued a square of Ultrasuede to the underside as a lining. I also embellished another square and stitched it to the top of the lid. If you'd like, add a decorative beaded handle, beaded feet, or any other type of detail you'd like.

Figure 4

chapter seven

BEADING FOR REMEMBRANCE

The need to tell stories and share information led people to develop writing—a system of encoding ideas in pictures or symbols. For many, beadwork is also a form of writing—a system of encoding ideas in colors and patterns. Beaded "words," just as if set in stone, carry additional weight. They can endure for generations, serving as a check on the fragility of life and memory.

The Luba of the Democratic Republic of the Congo (Zaire) preserve their history, traditions, and beliefs in a *lukasa*, or memory board. Some of these small, handheld wooden boards are carved. Others are covered with iron pins, cowrie shells, and colored beads.

Only a privileged few can decipher the information hidden in the lukasa's colors and geometric patterns. The Mbudye, a secret society of men and women, interpret the designs to teach rulers about the Luba kingdom and culture. They read or sing the encoded wisdom of the ancestors and the

The Luba encode their oral history in a lukasa, *or memory board. Some boards are carved in the shape of a crocodile, symbol of the Luba, or a turtle, symbol of a royal ancestress. Others have the shape of a female form—which the Luba consider a spiritually powerful and protective container for their sacred knowledge.* Photo courtesy of the UCLA Fowler Museum of Cultural History, collection of Suzanne K. Bennet. Photo by Done Cole (13½" [34 cm]).

stories of former kings, migrations, and sacred places. The Luba believe the gods provide the intricate designs.

Early Native American peoples of the northeast regions created their "documents" with white and purple shell beads called wampum. They strung and wove the cylindrical beads, made from whelk and quahog shells, into bracelets, collars, and belts. The word wampum means "white shell beads." The white whelk beads conveyed the ideas of peace and purity. Purple beads marked a serious matter or solemn event and often referred to ongoing or resolved hostilities. The purple quahog shell was difficult to drill, so purple wampum had great value.

Tribes communicated with each other and with the colonists through wampum belts. Having memorized the message in advance, a messenger would "read" the belt as he presented it—conveying its meaning in his own words and relying on the belt to aid his memory. A young man might send a wampum collar or necklace to the family of the woman he wished to marry. A go-between delivered the jewelry along with the intended message.

Wampum belts also commemorated significant tribal events, such as the signing of significant treaties. Disputes were not officially settled until the parties exchanged belts. These gifts were not only gestures of friendship, they also implied acceptance of the terms of the settlement. The beaded bands solidified the spoken agreement and served as a permanent record of the pact so it would never be forgotten. Wampum belts were marks of tribal honor, symbols of the solemn giving of one's word.

The symbols in the belt had specific meaning for the makers. The motifs in the geometric designs and the amount and placement of each color conveyed information about the participants and the event. Depending on the circumstances, belts might contain circles, crosses, hatchets, parallel rows of straight lines, wigwams, or figures with joined hands. The length and width of the belt reflected the importance of the event.

The desire to remember—and to be remembered—is a strong human impulse. Just as ideas and events are preserved in beadwork, so are the lives and spirits of cherished and revered people. In many cultures, a beaded memorial object is both a tribute and a sign of personal regard.

In various African tribes, people wear portrait carvings of ancestors or honored members of the community. These amulets maintain an ongoing connection between the living and the dead. The wearer hopes to inherit the character and personality of the person represented.

The Yoruba consider twin children to be sacred. If one twin dies, the parents arrange for the carving of a wooden memorial figure. They feed, clothe, and care for the wooden figure to express their love and respect for the child and their hope that its spirit will be born again. They often dress the carved figure in garments and jewelry made of beads and cowrie shells. Red and white beads honor the deity associated with twins.

For the ancient Egyptians, the scarab beetle signified spiritual transformation. The hieroglyphic for scarab means "to become." The scarab was featured in rings, amulets, and royal seals. Some scarabs were inscribed with names, dates, and symbols to commemorate members of royalty and significant historical events. They were also featured in religious ceremonies and depicted on coffins as symbols of immortality. Winged and heart scarabs, often of lapis or faience, were buried with mummified remains to ensure that the deceased would live a long life in the next world.

By sharing stories and preserving memories—whether with words or beads—we make our own talismans of immortality. We bring our ideas and emotions into tangible, lasting form. We forge our spiritual connections to each other and to those who came before. And by leaving these physical traces of ourselves for those who come after, we hold out the unfinished end of a long spirit strand.

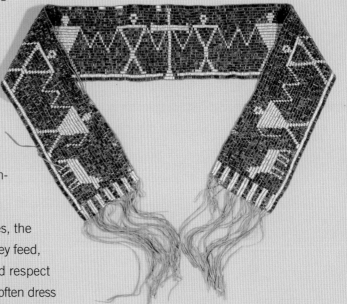

This wampum belt is known as the Two Dog Wampum. It commemorates the founding of the Mohawk community of Kahnesatà:ke at the Lake of Two Mountains near Oka, Quebec, Canada, in the late eighteenth century. The central cross represents the French people. The figures with joined hands represent the agreement made between the French and the native people for peaceful coexistence. Displayed with permission of the Kahnesatà:ke Cultural Centre. Photo courtesy of the McCord Museum of Natural History.

PERSONAL SYMBOLS NECKBAND

Diane Fitzgerald

"The inspiration for this neckband comes from the concept behind the memory boards of the Luba people of the Democratic Republic of the Congo (Zaire). Memory boards, which are called *lukasa*, are palm-sized wooden objects that represent the history of the Luba people, the stories of their ancestors, and the locations of local chiefdoms.

"Each lukasa is unique. These hand-carved wooden sculptures are often embellished with beads, pieces of coral, ivory, bone, shells, or even nails. In this way, history, religious beliefs, and cultural stories are translated into the designs and symbols of a secret code and exhibited for all to see but only a few to 'read.' (The boards belong to a council of men and women who sustain the political and historical principles of the Luba people.) In the absence of writing, the memory boards help the Luba people preserve oral tradition and remember their history.

"This concept of symbols as a key to trigger memory intrigued me. Do the symbols on a memory board differ greatly from the written word on a page? I applied the concept to my beadwork, weaving a system of my personal symbols into a simple necklace to represent my family history—for me and for no one else, a secret society of one. The designs flow easily from one to another or, at times, are discrete areas set off from what came before or what follows. Some patterns appear to be layered, others create optical illusions. But, just as people do, the designs begin and end, are intertwined and interrelated, and mutually coexist.

"I created the symbols in the neckband without a pattern, working with a palette of ten colors in diagonal brick stitch. As a result, there was no tedious counting or comparison to an existing chart, with the usual errors and removal of beads and stitches. It was uniquely satisfying to be so free as I worked and yet so bound up in thoughts of my family. I chose diagonal brick stitch because it creates a smooth edge, and patterns come easier to me with the level rows made by this stitch than with the offset rows of peyote stitch. The band can be made as a necklace or bracelet."

MATERIALS

Cylinder beads (Miyuki Delicas or Toho Treasures or Aikos), in assorted colors (about 250 beads per inch)

Nymo D thread

Synthetic beeswax

2 small clothing snaps

TOOLS

Size 10 beading needle

Small, sharp scissors

TECHNIQUES

Brick stitch variation

CREATING A DOUBLE-ROW BASE

You will create a band of brick stitch, 1" (2.5 cm) wide and about 20 to 24" (51 to 61 cm) long if you are making a necklace, 7 to 7½" (18 to 19 cm) long if you are making a bracelet.

Making a double-row base is an efficient way to start diagonal brick stitch because you are doing the first two rows at the same time. The method may remind you of the method for peyote stitch. These instructions are for rows that are 1 bead tall. Work with soft tension!

Begin with 1½ yd (137 cm) of a single strand of thread in the needle. Wax the thread lightly.

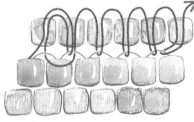

Figure 1

Figure 2

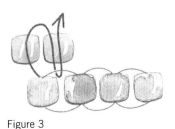

Figure 3

Rows 1 and 2: String 3 beads, leaving a 4" (10 cm) tail. Pass back through the first bead. Position the beads so they form a T and tie the working thread to the tail.

String 1 bead and pass back through the third bead you added in Step 1. String 1 bead and pass back through the last bead you added (Figure 1). Continue stringing 1 bead and passing back through the last bead added. Work until there are 15 beads across each of the two rows.

DIAGONAL BRICK STITCH

Diagonal brick stitch is worked like ordinary brick stitch, but a pattern of decreases and increases at the edges of each row creates a diagonal effect. Turn the work at the end of each row so that you are always working left to right.

Row 3: Begin this row by decreasing. Doing so will make the edge of the row you are working look indented. Add 2 beads. Pass the thread from back to front under the second loop in the previous row and up through the second bead just added. The beads will tilt a bit, so you'll need to lock the stitch. Pass down through the first bead just added and up through the second (Figure 2).

Work 12 brick stitches across the row, one in each loop, and increase at the end of the row. To make an increase at the end of a row, put an extra bead in the last loop (Figure 2).

Row 4: This row begins with an increase. To make an increase at the beginning of a row, add 2 beads, then pass the thread under the first loop in the previous row. Doing so will make the edge of the row you are working extend beyond the edge of the previous row (Figure 3). Work 13 brick stitches across the row, one in each loop. Do not increase at the end of the row.

Continue to repeat Rows 3 and 4, increasing and decreasing as indicated for the desired length of the piece.

To close the necklace, I overlapped the ends and sewed on two small clothing snaps. This type of closure works well for a bracelet, too.

TOTEM NECKLACE

Chelle Mayer

"When I was about three years old, I had a little box filled with buttons from my mom, grandmom, and great-grandmom. I had so much fun arranging and rearranging those buttons. Eventually I realized, much to the dismay of the grown-ups, that there was string in all the shoes scattered about the house—string, which, if I knotted it together in really neat patterns with the buttons, I could make into things to hang on my neck and wrists and head. So much fun! Right up there with jumping in rain puddles and squishing in clay!

"Years later, the container on my desk of stones, sparkly things, mementoes, and charms has the same appeal for me as those buttons. I constantly fiddle with them, and I was assembling and reassembling this necklace in my mind when I realized that I needed (okay, wanted) more beads, stones, and sparkly things. So I took the train down to New York City and wandered through bead shops where I found some pewter-colored and antique bronze-colored rocailles. As I held the beads in my hands, this piece suddenly came together for me. I purchased thread, needles, and beeswax so I could begin work right away.

"Once I was back on the train to Hudson, I abandoned the comfort of a mini couchlike seat for the hard flat seating in the dining car, where I created the pewter-and-bronze peyote-stitched band before I arrived home. I went straight to my desk to add the stone drops my brother brought back from Arizona, the stone I pulled from a sandy beach during my first trip to Boston, the gold stones I got while freelancing with an elegant Danish jeweler, the bits of blue sparkle that keep me close to the clouds and to the people I miss—it was like reading a new, captivating book whose ending I just can't wait to see.

"As I created this journal of wearable art, the memories of the mismatched button treasures came back to me, and I remembered plopping cross-legged in the foyer, pigtails bouncing off my head, knotting up shoe lacing and buttons while waiting for Papa so we could pick berries, draw cartoons, or feed the ducks. Making the necklace was just as satisfying as wearing it. It continually conjures up aspects of myself during the many adventures I

MATERIALS

Size 11° seed beads in pewter, bronze, and faceted gold

Stone chips and shapes (mine are a reminder of the first beaded necklace I bought)

Old key (a symbol of my willingness to seek and receive answers)

Lion charm (because I am a Leo)

Star of David (to honor Papa and our heritage)

Stone (which I found by the river)

Fetish stone (from a friend)

Stainless-steel teardrops (a reference to cleansing and renewing)

Chinese peace charm (that my brother brought back from his travels)

Round and bicone Swarovski crystals in sky and cloud colors (my children and I look up to the sky when we miss each other so we don't feel so far apart)

Geode slice (from Woodstock, New York)

Brass swing-latch clasp

Size D Nymo (or favorite thread) in color of your choice

Clear fingernail polish

TOOLS

Size 13 needle (and smaller if needed)

Thread Heaven thread conditioner or beeswax

Lighter

TECHNIQUES

Flat and tubular peyote stitch (page 153)

Fringes (page 154)

have had across the United States throughout my thirty-plus years. Each time I wear it, it brings me more memories to play with.

"I have listed the materials I used in my necklace but only as a reference. Make a piece that is about you and bits of your life, who you are, and where you have been. Pull out that container tucked away in your jewelry or underwear drawer—full of charms, stones, and coins waiting to be played with again—and dance with the thoughts and memories attached to your own treasures to create an authentic personal totem.

"This neckpiece is also a conversation piece, and it continues to create memories for me. I have formed friendships with strangers who comment on it. Our conversations took off, and now I have several new, special people in my life."

To make the band, thread the needle with two arm-lengths of thread. Use a contrasting bead to make a tension bead. Work in three-drop even-count peyote stitch. Make the first row by picking up 1 pewter, 1 gold, 2 pewter, 1 gold, and 1 pewter. Pick up 1 pewter, 1 gold, and 1 pewter. Skip 3 beads on the first row and pass through the remaining 3 beads to create half of the second row. Pick up 1 pewter, 1 gold, and 1 pewter, and pass through the three beads on top of the first row to complete the second row (Figure 1). Continue the band until it is a comfortable length—mine is 14" (35.5 cm). You now have a glass ribbon (feels neat, doesn't it?).

To attach the clasp, start a new thread that exits from an outside bead on the last row of the band. String 11 beads, alternating pewter and gold seed beads. Pass through the loop on the clasp. Pass back through the last row of the band, opposite the end where the thread last

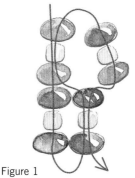

Figure 1

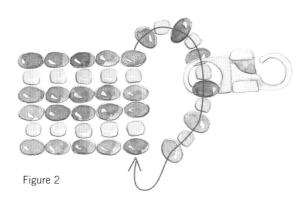

Figure 2

exited (Figure 2). Pass through all again twice more to reinforce.

To create the scalloped edge, pass through the last row of 6 beads, opposite the end the thread exits, so you are working on the inside edge. String 3 seed beads and pass through the second row of 6 beads and up through the next row of 6. Continue to create 3-bead scallops along the entire edge of the band.

Remove the tension bead. With the thread exiting the last row of 6 beads, string 11 beads to make a loop like the one on the other end of the band, with-

out the clasp. Lightly coat both loops with clear nail polish and let dry.

Now add your stones, crystals, and charms. Pour your container of treasures onto your work surface. Lay the band down and arrange them until you find the look and balance you like. To create the dangles, start a new thread at the last row on the unscalloped edge of the band. String 3 pewter, 4 or more seed beads, the treasure, and at least 4 seed beads. Pass back through the seed bead closest to the treasure, and through all the beads in the dangle except for the last 2 pewter beads. Pick up 2 pewter and pass up through the bead in the edge of the band.

Pass down through the adjacent bead in the band. Continue adding dangles of varying lengths. Get as funky as you want. Make the necklace yours—and have fun!

When you have added charms to half the necklace, set the work aside. Choose the treasure you want to feature as a central pendant (mine is a key). Start a new thread and work a small length of tubular peyote stitch around the treasure.

Add dangles to the beads you stitched around the pendant. Attach the central pendant to the band so it is centered on the front of the necklace.

Continue where you left off making dangles to finish the rest of the necklace.

Weave all thread tails into the necklace and trim each to $\frac{1}{8}$" (3 mm). Add clear nail polish to the knots, let dry, and carefully melt the exposed ends with a lighter.

TWO SCARAB BROOCHES

Judith Bennett

"From early childhood, I have had a sense of wonder about nature in general and insects in particular. As a child I searched for insects under leaves in a vacant lot. As an adult I have sought and collected antiques that depict insects—jewelry, wall pockets, ceramics, and especially, scarabs. Insects give me a feeling of connectedness to the ancient past, recent past, present, and future. They have outlived the dinosaurs and, for me, represent survival and the continuum of life.

"Found in the ancient tombs of the Egyptian pharaohs, scarabs have a special mystique. Through the years, I have collected old, art-glass scarabs—some genuine Tiffany glass, others Czech, still others of unknown origin. It has been an exciting hunt that has taken me to strange places—musty basements, abandoned warehouses filled with dusty, disintegrating cardboard boxes—each another sort of tomb.

"Each scarab I have discovered is distinctive in color, design, texture, and characteristic qualities, and I decided to design a series of brooches to interpret the various ideas that these individual stones suggest to me. I have always felt a connection to the civilization that believed them to be significant. How could I translate and reinterpret their ancient meanings to create original, modern pieces?

"As I developed my designs, I incorporated my sense of honor and respect for the scarab of the distant past and for re-creations from the less distant past. These two brooches are both winged scarabs, the type that the Egyptians believed would provide the soul with a safe journey to the afterworld. The designs are strong, the pieces large. Their drama and dimension convey their power.

"Preserving old scarabs—and buttons, buckles, beads, and other antique objects—has great significance for me. These small items are survivors of lost civilizations. The people may be long gone, but their artifacts remain. When I create my pieces, I work with the hope that they will survive long into the future. I hope that they become artifacts, too, and provide evidence that I was here."

MATERIALS

To make either brooch

Lightweight cardboard

2 pieces of 3½" (9 cm) wide medium-weight leather (metallized if desired)

1–1¼" (2.5–3.2 cm) scarab cabochon

Glass cabochons of assorted colors and sizes

Seed beads of assorted colors and sizes

Glass or metal vintage sew-ons

Bugle beads, crystals, and other decorative elements

Pin back

Nymo D or other beading thread

E-6000 glue

Thin 3 × 4" piece of plastic (as in a salad bar take-out container)

Toothpicks

TOOLS

Pencil or fine marker

Small, curved blade scissors

Size 10 or 12 sharp needles

Razor blade, X-acto knife, or ⅛" (3 mm) elliptical hole punch

Thin nail file

Emery board

TECHNIQUES

Creating bezels

Backstitch (page 155)

Design a brooch shape and draw it on the cardboard. Cut out the shape and trace it onto a piece of leather. Cut out the leather shape, making it slightly larger than the traced line.

Position the scarab cabochon on the leather and trace around it, following its contour closely. Remove the cabochon and backstitch one round of seed beads along the traced line to create a bezel. Do not remove the needle and thread from the leather.

With a toothpick, apply glue to the area within the bezel and to the back of the cabochon. Let the glue set for five to ten minutes and then gently position the cab within the bezel.

Weave through the seed beads several times, pulling the row tight so that the beads hug the cab. If desired, extend the bezel with two or three rounds of peyote stitch. Create additional rows of seed beads around the base of the bezel to emphasize the cab.

Following your own design, add cabochons throughout the piece, creating bezels as desired. Fill in the areas between the cabs by stitching on bugle beads, sew-ons, crystals, seed beads, or other elements.

Now trim away the excess leather to create the final shape of the brooch. Be careful not to cut any stitches.

Trace the leather brooch onto the piece of plastic. Cut the plastic about ½" (1.3 cm) smaller than the leather along all edges. Adhere the plastic to the back of the leather by applying glue to both surfaces. Rub and squeeze the surfaces together to eliminate any air bubbles that may be trapped between them.

Glue the pin back to the plastic above the midline of the brooch. To create the backing, trace the shape of the brooch onto the second piece of leather. Cut the backing roughly to shape so that it is slightly larger than the brooch.

Punch a hole or make a small crosscut in the leather backing with the razor or X-acto to serve as the opening for the

hinged end of the pin. Insert the pin through the opening to check the fit. Mark the spot for the clasp end of the pin on the inside of the leather. Remove the leather piece and cut out or punch the second hole.

Insert the pin through the leather backing, checking to ensure that the spacing is correct and the pin will close. Adhere the leather backing to the plastic by applying glue to both surfaces (Figure 1). Press firmly all across the surface to bond. Again, rub and squeeze the surfaces to eliminate trapped air bubbles. Work the leather with the nail file so that it is as flat as possible around the hinge and the clasp.

Trim any excess leather so that the back and front of the brooch are identical in size. Carefully smooth any rough edges of the leather with the emery board. You can also finish the edges with a beaded picot stitch if desired.

gallery

EYE OF TURQUOISE (III)

Margi Foster

"My intention when I conceived this design was to aid empowerment—so that the wearer would be fortified against any feeling of weakness or fear of malevolent influences, would indeed 'see' or sense their approach through the power portal provided by the large central amulet, and would marshal inner resources to meet the challenge, perhaps reassured by the abundant protection that the piece itself provides.

"Turquoise looks—and feels—elemental. It creates a powerful and immediate link between the wearer and the earth—an effect that is much more empowering than that created by other gem materials.

"Turquoise is often worn in great profusion, layers upon layers, to augment the feeling of power and protection. The resulting weight promotes a great sense of grounding and oneness with the earth. The overall effect can be stunning—in fact awe-inspiring! Would this piece not stop a malevolent spirit dead in its tracks?"

BEAUTY IN THE EYE OF THE BEHOLDER

Laura McCabe

"I have recently created a series of eye jewelry that utilizes glass doll and animal eyes and human prosthetic eyes. The intended impact on the viewer is one of alarm and intrigue, because the more intense and real the image of the eye, the more effective it will be in warding off ill will.

"The realistic prosthetic eyes make Beauty in the Eye of the Beholder quite startling. The three eyes in the centerpiece and the one positioned at the back as the closure are human prosthetics dating from the First World War. The small eyes in the neck strap are from antique dolls. This piece also incorporates the ancient magical numbers three, seven, and nine. There are three eyes in the centerpiece. If you count the eye closure and the doll eyes in the neck strap, they total nine. All the little embellishments on the neck strap are also derived from these numbers."

Photo by Joanne Schmaltz.

THE BEAD QUILT PROJECT

Team BeadQuilt

"The Bead Quilt Project *remains an enduring tribute to the events of September 11, 2001, and how they touched our world. When we began the project, none of us was sure if it could really make a difference—but members of the beading community united to give it a try.*

"As the squares started to come in, we saw how making them really helped the artists cope with their feelings about the attacks. What's surprising is the way that this healing effect continues to ripple out as people view the quilts. Each exhibit has been emotional and powerful—sometimes viewers weep quietly as they look at the squares and read the accompanying statements. Other people chat with strangers next to them about how wonderful it makes them feel to see such an overwhelming show of strength and positivity.

"This project encompasses a full range of ideas, emotions, and voices from around the globe, united to create a single message of hope."

Photo by Julia Pretl.

SPOOLS AND TRIANGLE

Penny Harrell

Penny Harrell died just weeks before she was to be invited to participate in the making of this book. Yet, with the help of her husband Jim, Penny's strong spirit—which filled and was nourished by her beadwork during the years she struggled with illness—still graces these pages as testimony to the powerful role of beadwork in the very personal process of healing psyche and soul.

"In 1989, while being treated for breast cancer, I woke one morning thinking 'Life may be short so I better get on with doing what pleases me most.' I started making bolo ties on the family-room floor. Gradually, beadwork has taken over my life (and Jim's), and we couldn't be happier.

"In the beginning, I drew charts of my designs. Now I create each piece in hand. I find great pleasure exploring surface and color possibilities. The moment when a new texture or subtle color combination comes alive is exquisite and sustains me for a very long time."

DIG DEEPER

Julia Pretl

"I first saw Egyptian broadcollars in Virginia Blakelock's book Those Bad, Bad Beads! and was instantly drawn to them. They are romantic and powerful and allow me to push aside my ever-practical self and create something completely impractical. Beadwork is a building process and, metaphorically speaking, broadcollars allow me to build castles instead of houses.

"At the time I began Dig Deeper, I was struggling to make my beadwork express my emotions rather than just look nice. I felt the need to say something—but was not sure what it was or how to say it. The solution was right in front of me. I would make a piece that reflected my need to 'dig deeper.'

"I decided to begin with the focal point—the heart of the matter, so to speak. I chose bead embroidery because I don't normally associate this technique with broadcollars and hoped it would push my boundaries a bit. Once complete, the heart was warm and full of life. I had succeeded.

"Feeling the need to return to my comfort zone, I began the ladder. Back with calculations and methodical construction, I felt at ease again. By the time I reached the fringe (always my favorite part), I was finally able to break free. This finishing touch allowed me to express myself perfectly—staid, practical fringe around the boundaries and wild, expressive branches flowing from the heart."

SNAKE NECKLACE

Sage Holland

"This snake necklace was made with the movements of a live snake in mind. It is an articulated sculpture as much as it is a wearable piece. The necklace is worn with its head biting its tail around the front of the wearer's chest. The form recalls the ancient concept of the snake as the symbol of the cosmos, an unbroken circle. The pagan cultures of ancient Europe felt the snake's power was female in principle and that the snake had the gift of resurrection through the shedding of its skin.

"I love snakes because they live in little holes in the ground or under a rock and they are so beautiful yet can be so poisonous. They make you acutely aware of where you're stepping as you walk through life's wilderness.

"The fact that many people have a fear of snakes gives the wearer of this necklace the opportunity to confront her own fears—and the fears of those who observe the snake while she is wearing it. I feel that one of the big reasons we're here on this planet is to confront and dispel ancient, primal fears."

Courtesy of Joan Flesch.

RAINFOREST NECKLACES

Isis Ray

"Our planet is so beautiful and so full of diversity. We are allowing much of that diversity to be destroyed, never to be replaced. This concern motivates me to create objects that capture some of Earth's wilderness as talismans for the future and to promote awareness of the delicate balance in nature. These necklaces are meant to evoke a reverence for Earth, nature, and diversity, and respect for the Native American spirituality that is so closely connected to nature.

"Spirits of the Northwest Rainforest *features a murrine bead (made with slices of fused-glass mosaics) that represents ferns, spawning sockeye salmon, and a traditional design element from a native Chilkat woven blanket. On the back, I painted a masked native Alaskan figure and an old-growth tree. The necklace also contains whiteheart seed beads, Russian blues, dentalium shells, and abalone beads.*

"The focal bead in Spirits of the Tropical Rainforest *features a painting of a jaguar, flowers, and an individual murrina (mosaic) of an 88 butterfly—a species with markings resembling the number 88 on its wings. This necklace also contains lampworked beads, garnets, and carved stone flower beads."*

CELEBRATING SARAH

Judith Bennett

"My niece learned that a favorite professor of hers, a past president of the Button Society, had amassed a large collection of antique buttons. The professor agreed to meet with me, and I was delighted to drive five hours (each way) for a private viewing.

"He and I talked for hours. He then opened a drawer and withdrew a gilded buckle that had been Sarah Bernhardt's. 'You should have this,' he said. 'It belongs with you.'

Much of my creative process is infusing old objects with new life. I never alter or harm the originals, because I feel a strong responsibility to their integrity. I try to honor and respect them in the form in which they were created.

"I designed the necklace around a matched set of rare, domed, French-enameled buttons that the professor and I found in his collection. I added tiny, vintage Swarovski crystals by the score and microscopic steel-cut French beads, which I had gold-plated. I chose subtle colors and a symmetrical design to showcase the Divine Sarah, the turn-of-the-century actress who dared to play Hamlet. Wearing this neckpiece is itself a celebration. I think Sarah would be pleased."

IN KRISHNA'S FOOTSTEPS

Helen Banes

"This necklace was inspired by a Hindu amulet of the footsteps of Krishna, which my daughter brought me from India. In the Bhagavad Gita, one of India's sacred books, the lord Krishna advises a disciple seeking enlightenment to follow in the footsteps of other disciples who have followed him. Every year, on Krishna's birthday, devoted Hindus decorate their houses with patterns of small white footprints, drawn with rice-flour paste, to represent the footsteps of the baby Krishna who has come into their homes to bless them.

"The colors of the amulet influenced my choice of colors for the weaving threads and for the beads of various shapes: rose for the background, with deep purple lines leading to the circle, and metallic silver threads that repeat the silver in the amulet frame."

THE BEADED PRAYERS PROJECT

Sonya Clark

"I created the concept of The Beaded Prayers Project. Inspired by the worldwide traditions in which powerful prayers and 'medicines' are enclosed in amulets, I asked participants to write down their wishes, prayers, or aspirations on a small sheet of paper. They then folded and stitched or sealed the papers in packets, which they decorated with beads. I asked participants to make two copies of their beaded prayers, so that they could each keep one and contribute the other to the traveling exhibit.

"Since then, the project has grown, and more than 4,000 people—ages six to ninety—from thirty-five nations have contributed. The traveling exhibit, Beaded Blessings, contains more than seventy two-foot-square panels. People are able to add prayers only at the exhibit venues, but I encourage others to start their own beaded prayer collections."

Courtesy of The Baltimore Museum of Art. Photo by Cliff Dossel.

CHURCH FANS

David Dean

"I learned to make traditional fans from elder Kiowa and Comanche fan builders. Many of these artists were followers of the teachings of the Native American Church of North America, where fans are instruments for prayer. The feathers signify that prayers are being carried to the Creator on the wings of birds. The fan builder must pray for this intention as he builds the fan.

"Before I begin work, I interview the person who will own the fan. Many of the design elements and color combinations may come out of an experience the owner had during a church ceremony.

"Each beaded piece I make carries with it the spirit and inspiration of all the artists whose work I have studied. Attention to detail, inspiration from those who have gone before us, and the occasional prayer to the Creator are what it takes to create art that is true to tradition and inspirational to others."

MOROCCAN AMMONITE NECKLACE

Mary Hicklin

"My home and business were destroyed in the first hours of the Cedar Fire in San Diego in 2003. Within less than ten minutes after I woke up, my hillside exploded in flames. I was extremely fortunate to escape without injury. I saved only my little truck, a dresser drawer with a bit of jewelry, and a photo of my mom.

"In the weeks and months that followed, I was overwhelmed by generosity. Friends and strangers sent boxes of well-loved beads from their collections, handmade beads, antiques, and every color of 15° available. These gifts gave me what I needed to resume the work I love. This necklace includes the 'love beads' sent by those friends and strangers, and the necklace carries the energy of their loving concern. I can never repay their kindness. I hope they know that every time I pick up a tool or a bead they sent, I am deeply thankful."

Photo by Melinda Holden.

TREASURE PEOPLE

Penny Harrell

"It is natural that we create diverse cultures based on the land, food, plants, and history we inherit. Our cultures make us appear very different—yet we all love, laugh, dance, cry, and sing. Treasure People express this 'one-people' aspect of being human. I've made Jamaican dancers, cheerleaders, farmers and fisherman, Manchu kings, African warriors, and practically everything in between.

"I have also learned (or understood or imagined) that these funny little people come from the Lost Civilization of Abundanza, where everyone is born with an abundance of talent and a generous spirit. In order to keep that talent, they need to share it.

"So, along about sundown, everyone in town gathers at the well, arms outstretched, offering the gifts of their talent to anyone in need. Although it is considered a kindness to accept any gifts one can use, the person with a genuine need is most highly valued. For a gift to someone in need ensures that the giver will continue to have talent. So it is in this fictional Lost Civilization of Abundanza that no one is hungry and no one is ashamed.

"The treasure people leave my hands and travel all around the world, spreading their generosity wherever they go."

PROMISE

Sonya Clark

"In my beaded work, I am actively engaged in remembering. My hands have the unique wisdom of knowing beads. Early in the process of learning a technique, the head trains the hand, but eventually the hand becomes the master, and the head steps out of the process, which becomes meditative. My body understands the subtlety of its relationship with material and process in a way that is impossible for my head to imagine.

"Beadwork is a metaphor for community. I often think of each bead as an individual. Stitched together, these individual beads form a community. The objects I make are symbols to remind us of our individual heritages and shared responsibility to one another. A promise is only valuable if it is remembered. This piece was made as a promise to remember all the hands that have crafted objects and lovingly cared for us."

Photo by Tom McInvaille.

WALK ON THE BEACH

Stephanie Sersich

"This necklace is the natural expression of my desire to remember Costa Rica, the most romantic and beautiful place I've ever visited. I plucked all the shells in this piece from the sands of the country's most dynamic beach, Playa Guiones in Nosara. The color palette is taken directly from the one that nature made. All I had to do was find the shells, put them together with the lampworked glass beads I made to go with them, and then add the other elements that fortify my memories.

"Nosara is renowned for its dramatic surf, so I incorporated the loops of blue to recall those relentless waves. The circles and spheres will always remind me of the sunsets there. With what I call my spiny knotting technique, which binds together all the pieces, I created decorative fiber work that has both a nautical and natural feeling."

Photo by R. Diamante.

Photo by Joanne Schmaltz.

MR. P

Alison Pyott

"Mr. P lived with me for eleven years. I always thought he was really a wise old monk, moving through the world in a beautiful dog costume. He never seemed like just a dog to me or to most of the people he met in his travels.

"P Dog taught me a myriad of lessons in our time together, mostly about love and simplicity and about being more truthful and trustworthy in my life. When he got older and developed health problems, these lessons became more poignant as I became aware that at some point he'd be moving on.

"Mr. P died in August 2003 at the end of a beautiful last week we spent together. A few weeks later, I was sitting on the back steps, my hands in the bag of his ashes, the last little bit of his material nature left to me. It was such an organic mix: sandy, gray, ashy grains and a few pieces of bone or tooth. I had expected something more ephemeral.

"This necklace holds three pieces of that bone, which are enclosed by the largest clusters of pearls. I designed the necklace to hold his relics near a very vulnerable part of my body (the hollow of my neck). The berrylike fruits hold seeds of new life. The necklace is a talisman of transformation, companionship, and deep love. I take this little essence of Mr. P with me wherever I go—and people notice it, just like they noticed him. In fact, I think they are still noticing the beauty of my dear friend, and not really the necklace at all."

9/11 MEMORIAL WREATHS

Dalene Isobel Kelly (project initiator)

Marlene Didner (coordinator of the Pennsylvania wreath)

Estelle Johnson (coordinator of the Pentagon wreath)

Deborah Zabel (coordinator of the World Trade Center wreath)

In keeping with the long tradition of creating memorial wreaths, a group of bead artists came together in a gesture of tribute and remembrance to the men and women lost on September 11, 2001. After sharing ideas through their online forum (beadedflowers@yahoogroups.com), hundreds of bead artists throughout the United States, Australia, Canada, England, France, Italy, and Switzerland contributed flowers and stems of greenery they created with French and Victorian beaded flower techniques. Volunteers spent thousand of hours assembling the flowers to create three wreaths—one to honor those at each of the three crash sites.

The Pennsylvania wreath is on permanent display at the National Liberty Museum in Philadelphia. The Pentagon wreath is part of a memorial display at the Pentagon in Washington, D.C., although it's not available for public viewing. The World Trade Center wreath, which was for a time displayed at the Museum of American Glass at Wheaton Village in Millville, New Jersey, does not yet have a permanent home.

Pentagon wreath. Photo by Tod Cohen. Courtesy of Carol Benner Doelp.

World Trade Center wreath. Photo by Stephan Harrison. Courtesy of Deborah Zabel.

Pennsylvania wreath. Photo by James Dowell. Courtesy of Marlene Didner.

KNOTS

SLIPKNOT

With the end of the stringing material in your palm, wrap the working yarn around your index and middle fingers, and lay the working stringing material across the tail end, forming an X (Figure 1). Spread your fingers slightly and push the working stringing material through your fingers from the back of your hand. Pull this loop up slightly while holding the tail end of the stringing material to form a knot (Figure 2).

Figure 1

Figure 2

SQUARE

This is the classic knot for securing most stringing materials. First make an overhand knot, passing the right end over the left end. Next, make another overhand knot, this time passing the left end over the right end. Pull tight.

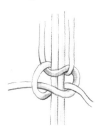

LARK'S HEAD

Begin by folding the stringing material in half. Bend the fold over the bar (Figure 1). Pull the ends through the loop and tighten (Figure 2).

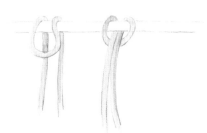

Figure 1   Figure 2

OVERHAND

Make a loop with the stringing material. Pass the cord that lies behind the loop over the front cord and through the loop. Pull tight.

SURGEON'S

Tie an overhand knot, right over left, but instead of one twist over the left cord, make at least two. Tie another overhand knot, left over right, and pull tight.

HALF HITCH

The half hitch may be worked with two or more strands—one strand is knotted over one or more other strands. The knot may be worked from right to left, left to right, or in a combination of the two. Use it to make a clasp for a choker or necklace by tying a half-hitched loop in the cord before you start knotting with beads. When you've finished the piece, attach a bead or make a knot of the appropriate size to fit through the loop like a button.

OFF-LOOM STITCHES

Note: When you're reading off-loom beading instructions, *pass through* means to move the needle in the same direction that the beads have been strung. *Pass back through* means to move the needle in the opposite direction.

FINISHING AND STARTING NEW THREADS

Tie off an old thread when it's about 4" (10 cm) long by making a simple knot between beads. Pass through a few beads and pull tight to hide the knot. Weave through a few more beads and trim the thread close to the work.

Start the new thread by tying a knot between beads and weaving through a few beads. Pull tight to hide the knot. Weave through several beads until you reach the place to resume beading.

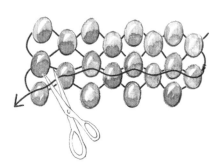

TENSION BEAD

Use a tension bead (or stopper bead) while you're doing off-loom beadwork to hold the work in place. To make a tension bead, string a bead larger than those you are working with, then pass through this bead one or more times, making sure not to split the thread. The bead will be able to slide along, but will still provide tension to work against when you're beading the first rows.

BRICK STITCH

Begin by creating a foundation row in ladder stitch. String one bead and pass under the closest exposed loop of the foundation row. Pass back through the same bead and continue across, adding one bead at a time.

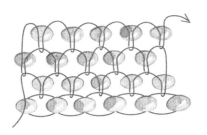

LADDER STITCH

Using two needles, one threaded on each end of the thread, pass one needle through one or more beads from left to right and pass the other needle through the same beads from right to left. Continue adding beads by crisscrossing both needles through each bead or bead group. Use this stitch to make strings of beads or to lay the foundation for brick stitch.

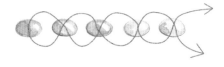

For a single-needle ladder, string two beads and pass through them again. String one bead. Pass through the last stitched bead and the one just strung. Repeat, adding one bead at a time and working in a figure-eight pattern.

PEYOTE STITCH

Peyote stitch is usually worked one bead at a time, but it is also common to see it done with up to three beads per stitch.

Even-count flat peyote stitch

Begin by stringing an even number of beads, twice the number you want in one row. These beads will become the first and second rows. Create the next row by stringing one bead and passing through the second-to-last bead of the previous row. String another bead and pass through the fourth-to-last bead of the previous row. Continue adding one bead at a time, passing over every other bead of the previous row.

Tubular peyote stitch

This technique is easiest when worked tightly around a cylindrical form like a dowel. Begin by stringing an even number of beads and make a foundation circle by passing through them two more times, exiting from the first bead strung (Figure 1). String one bead and pass through the third bead of the foundation circle. String one bead and pass through the fifth bead of the foundation circle. Continue adding one bead at a time, skipping over one bead in the first round, until you have added half the number of beads of the first round. Exit from the first bead of the second round (Figure 2). String one bead, pass

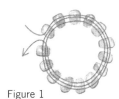

Figure 1

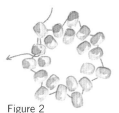

Figure 2

Figure 3

through the second bead added in the second round, and pull the thread very tight so the beads form a tube. String one bead and pass through the third bead added in the second round. Continue around, filling in the "spaces" one bead at a time (Figure 3). Exit from the first bead added in each round to step up and start the next round.

WIREWORK

WRAPPED LOOP

Use a flat- or chain-nose pliers to make a 90° bend in the wire 2" (5 cm) from one end. Use a round-nose pliers to hold the wire near the angle and bend the short end up and around the pliers until the wire meets itself. Wrap the end tightly down the neck of the wire to create a couple of coils. Trim the excess close to the coils.

SIMPLE LOOP

Grasp one end of the wire with round-nose pliers. Holding on to the wire with one hand, gently turn the pliers until the wire end and wire body touch. Create a 90° reverse bend where they meet.

JUMP RINGS

Jump rings connect wirework to findings. When you open or close a jump ring, use two pliers and bend the ends laterally, not apart. Add the finding and close the jump ring with the two pliers. Be sure to close the jump ring completely so the finding doesn't slip out. Do so by closing the ends slightly farther than where the ends match up—the wire will spring back to the right position.

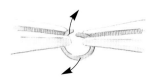

FRINGES

SIMPLE FRINGE

Anchor the thread in the fabric or bead-work base. String a length of beads plus one bead. Skipping the last bead, pass back through all the beads just strung to create a fringe leg. Pass back into the foundation row or fabric and repeat as desired (Figure 1). To make a leaflike fringe variation, string 6 beads, pass back through the fifth bead strung, string 3 beads, and pass back through the first bead strung (Figure 2).

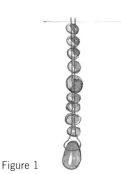

Figure 1

Figure 2

BRANCH FRINGE

Anchor the thread in the fabric or bead-work base. String fifteen or more beads. Skip the last bead and pass back through six beads just strung. String six to eight beads. Skip the last bead and pass back through the rest just strung. Pass back through six beads originally strung. String six to eight beads. Skip the last bead and pass back through the rest just strung. Pass up through the rest of the fringe leg and secure within the base.

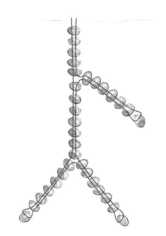

LOOPED FRINGE

Anchor the thread in the fabric or bead-work base. String a measured length of beads, form a loop, and stitch next to the first anchor spot. For each successive loop, string the same length of beads and pass it through the previous loop to interlace the loops before stitching the last loop to the edge.

BEAD EMBROIDERY

BACKSTITCH (also known as return stitch and running stitch)

Begin by passing the needle through the fabric from wrong side to right side, at the place where the first bead is to go. String a bead and pass the needle back through the fabric to the left of the bead. Bring the needle back through the fabric to the right of the bead, pass back through the bead, and back down through the fabric. Continue with one backstitch per bead. You can sew up to

three beads per stitch by stringing three beads and backstitching through only the third one.

LANE STITCH

Also known as lazy stitch, crow stitch, and spot stitch, it's one of the earliest techniques used by Native American beadworkers. The beads in each row should lie as close as possible to their neighbors without being crowded. It takes some practice to get even rows that lie flat.

Lane stitch #1. Begin by passing the needle through the fabric. String the desired number of beads, make a stitch in the cloth, string more beads, and repeat.

Lane stitch #2. This is essentially the same as lazy stitch #1 except that you end the row when you take a stitch. String the desired number of beads, make a stitch, string beads for the next row, and reverse direction.

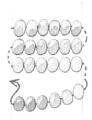

Spot stitch. Also known as couching, this technique uses two threaded needles. Begin by passing the needle through the fabric, from wrong side to right side, at the place where the first bead is to go. Thread a number of beads and lay them onto the cloth in your chosen design. With the second threaded needle, come up through the cloth, over the thread between two beads, and back down through the cloth. Repeat this procedure until all the beads lie flat.

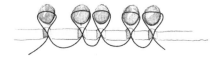

SEWING

WHIPSTITCH

Bring the needle up at 1, insert at 2, and bring up at 3. These quick basting-type stitches do not have to be very tight or close together.

MISCELLANEOUS

STRINGING BEADS

Use stringing material (needle and thread, beading wire, elastic, leather) to pass through the holes of beads.

CRIMPING

Crimping is the best way to secure beading wire to a clasp or other connector. To start, begin the strand of beads with a crimp tube. Pass through the clasp or connector. Pass back through the crimp tube and, if possible, a few beads on the strand. Snug the crimp tube and beads close to the closure. Spread the two wires so they line each side of the tube. Use the first notch on the crimping pliers (round on one jaw, dipped on the other) to squeeze the

crimp tube shut, making sure there's one wire on each side of the crimp (Figure 1). Use the second notch on the crimping pliers (rounded on both jaws) to shape the tube into a tight round (Figure 2). Make gentle squeezes around the tube for a perfect cylinder. Trim the tail wire close to the beads.

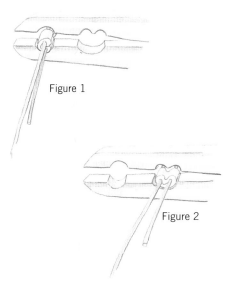

Figure 1

Figure 2

BRAIDING

Start with three strands of stringing material or three strands of strung beads that are knotted together at one end. Pass the right strand under the center strand (the right strand now becomes the center strand). Pass the left strand under the center strand. Continue for the desired length.

REFERENCES AND SUGGESTED READING

Ao, Ayinla Shilu. *Naga Tribal Adornment: Signatures of Status and Self.* Washington, D.C.: Bead Society of Greater Washington, 2003.

Arellano, Lee Price. "Chachales of Guatemalan Mayan Indians." *Ornament* 24, no. 1 (2000): 30–33.

Arnoldi, Mary Jo, and Christine Mullen Kreamer. *Crowning Achievements: African Arts of Dressing the Head.* Los Angeles: Fowler Museum of Cultural History, 1995.

Atkins, Robin. *One Bead at a Time: Exploring Creativity with Bead Embroidery.* Friday Harbor, Washington: Tiger Press, 2000.

Banes, Helen. *Fiber and Bead Jewelry.* With Sally Banes. New York: Sterling Publishing, 2002.

Banes, Helen, and Diane Fitzgerald. *Beads and Threads: A New Technique for Fiber Jewelry.* Gaithersburg, Maryland: Flower Valley Press, 1993.

Berrin, Kathleen, ed. *Art of the Huichol Indians.* New York: Harry N. Abrams, 1978.

Coles, Janet, and Robert Budwig. *World Beads: An Exploration of Bead Traditions Around the World.* New York: Simon and Schuster, 1997.

Crabtree, Carolyn, and Pam Stallebrass. *Beadwork: A World Guide.* New York: Rizzoli International Publications, 2002.

Dean, David. *Beading in the Native American Tradition.* Loveland, Colorado: Interweave Press, 2002.

Diamanti, Joyce. *Silver Speaks: Traditional Jewelry of the Middle East.* Washington, D.C.: The Bead Society of Greater Washington, 2002.

Dickt, Donna DeAngelis. *Designer Beadwork: French Beaded Flowers.* New York: Sterling, 2005.

Doelp, Carol Benner. *The Art of French Beaded Flowers.* Asheville, North Carolina: Lark, 2004.

Drewal, Henry John, and John Mason. *Beads, Body, and Soul: Art and Light in the Yoruba Universe.* Los Angeles: UCLA Fowler Museum of Cultural History, 1998.

Dubin, Lois Sherr. *The History of Beads from 30,000 B.C. to the Present.* New York: Harry N. Abrams, 1987.

———. *North American Indian Jewelry and Adornment.* New York: Harry N. Abrams, 1999.

Egan, Martha. *Milagros: Votive Offerings from the Americas.* Santa Fe: Museum of New Mexico Press, 1991.

Erickson, Joan Mowat. *The Universal Bead.* New York: W. W. Norton, 1993.

Feest, Christian F. *Native Arts of North America.* New York: Oxford University Press, 1980.

Fisher, Angela. *Africa Adorned.* New York: Harry N. Abrams, 1984.

Fitzgerald, Diane. *Beading with Brick Stitch.* Loveland, Colorado: Interweave Press, 2001.

———. *Netted Beadwork.* Loveland, Colorado: Interweave Press, 2003.

Gillow, John, and Nicholas Barnard. *Traditional Indian Textiles.* London: Thames and Hudson, 1991.

d'Harcourt, Raoul. *Textiles of Ancient Peru and Their Techniques.* Seattle: University of Washington Press, 1962.

Hatanaka, Kokyo. *Textile Arts of India.* San Francisco: Chronicle Books, 1996.

Henry, Gray, and Susannah Marriott. *Beads of Faith.* London: Carroll and Brown, 2002.

Jenkins, Cindy. *Beads of Glass: The Art and the Artists.* St. Louis, Missouri: Pyro Press, 2004.

Kunz, George Frederick. *The Curious Lore of Precious Stones.* Philadelphia: J. B. Lippincott Company, 1913.

Liu, Robert K. *Collectible Beads: A Universal Aesthetic.* Vista, California: Ornament, 1995.

———. "Iranian Amulets." *Ornament* 7, no. 1 (1983): 59.

———. "Polynesian Leis." *Ornament* 27, no. 1 (2003): 52–53.

Markowitz, Yvonne, and Sheila Shear. "Ptahshepses Impy's Beaded Broadcollar." *Ornament* 26, no. 2 (2002/03): 70–73.

McManis, Kent. *Zuni Fetishes and Carvings.* Tucson: Rio Nuevo, 1998.

Moriarty, Linda Paik. *Ni'ihau Shell Leis.* Honolulu: University of Hawaii Press, 1986.

Morris, Jean, and Eleanor Preston-Whyte. *Speaking with Beads: Zulu Arts from Southern Africa.* New York: Thames and Hudson, 1994.

Mullin, Glenn H. *Female Buddhas: Women of Enlightenment in Tibetan Mystical Art.* With Jeff J. Watt. Santa Fe: Clearlight Publishers, 2003.

Nooter, Mary H. *Secrecy: African Art That Conceals and Reveals.* New York: Museum for African Art, 1993.

Oktavec, Eileen. *Answered Prayers: Miracles and Milagros across the Border.* Tucson: University of Arizona Press, 1995.

Painter, Dagmar. "Sacred and Potent: The Magic of Thai Amulets." *Ornament* 13, no. 4: 36–39.

Robinson, David. *Beautiful Death: Art of the Cemetery.* New York: Penguin Studio, 1996.

Sciama, Lidia D., and Joanne B. Eicher. *Beads and Bead Makers: Gender, Material Culture and Meaning.* New York: Berg, 1998.

Tobin, Jacqueline L., and Raymond G. Dobard, PhD. *Hidden in Plain View: A Secret Story of Quilts and the Underground Railroad.* New York: Doubleday, 1999.

Tomalin, Stefany. *The Bead Jewelry Book.* Chicago: NTC/Contemporary Publishing, 1998.

Wade, Edwin L., ed. *The Arts of the North American Indian.* New York: Hudson Hills Press, 1986.

Walker, Barbara G. *The Woman's Dictionary of Symbols and Sacred Objects.* New York: HarperSanFrancisco, 1988.

Wiley, Eleanor, and Maggie Oman Shannon. *A String and a Prayer: How to Make and Use Prayer Beads.* York Beach, Maine: Red Wheel, 2002.

SOURCES

BALLY BEAD COMPANY
2304 Ridge Rd.
Rockwall, TX 75087
(800) 543-0280
www.ballybead.com
(Jewelry making supplies)

THE BEAD GOES ON
PO Box 592
14 Church St.
Vineyard Haven
Martha's Vineyard, MA 02568
(866) 861-2323
www.beadgoeson.com
(Jewelry making beads and supplies)

THE BEADIN' PATH
15 Main St.
Freeport, ME 04032
(877) 922-3237
www.beadinpath.com
(Lampworked, silver, vintage, and gemstone beads)

GREEN GIRL STUDIOS
176 Flint St.
Asheville, NC 28801
(828) 255-8236
www.greengirlstudios.com
(Silver and pewter charms, milagros)

INDIAN JEWELERS SUPPLY COMPANY
601 E. Coal Ave.
Gallup, NM 87301-6005
(505) 722-4451
www.ijsinc.com
(Jewelry making supplies)

MICROSTAMP CORPORATION
2770 E. Walnut St.
Pasadena, CA 91107
(800) 243-3543
www.microstampusa.com
(Maker's tags, stamps)

THE MYKONOS
59 Amory St., Loft 401
Boston, MA 02119
(888) 695-6667
www.mykonosbeads.com
(Traditional Turkish eye beads)

RIO GRANDE
7500 Bluewater Rd. NW
Albuquerque, NM 87121-1962
(800) 545-6566
www.riogrande.com
(Jewelry making beads and supplies)

THE SOFT FLEX COMPANY
PO Box 80
Sonoma, CA 95476
(707) 938-3539
www.softflexcompany.com
(Stringing materials)

SOVA-ENTERPRISES
948 Eubank Blvd. NE
Albuquerque, NM 87112-5308
(877) 262-1369
www.sova-enterprises.com
(Bead backing)

STEPHANIE SERSICH
PO Box 11072
Portland, ME 04104
(207) 775-0870
(Lampworked beads)

TESOROS TRADING COMPANY
209 Congress Ave.
Austin, TX 78701
(512) 479-8377
www.tesoros.com/homepage.html
(Milagros)

ELEANOR WILEY
Contemporary Prayer Beads
1402 Santa Clara Ave.
Alameda, CA 94501
(510) 865-1349
www.prayerbdz.com
(Sacred Wheel of Peace, large and small, in brass, bronze, gold, sterling silver, and pewter)

INDEX